CW01011141

THE PIANO PLAYER IN
PLAYER IN
THE BROTHEL

THE PIANO PLAYER IN THE BROTHEL

THE FUTURE OF JOURNALISM

JUAN LUIS CEBRIÁN

TRANSLATED FROM THE SPANISH BY EDUARDO SCHMID

INTRODUCTION BY HAROLD EVANS

OVERLOOK DUCKWORTH
NEW YORK · LONDON

This edition first published in the United States and the United Kingdom
in 2011 by Overlook Duckworth, Peter Mayer Publishers, Inc.

NEW YORK:
Overlook
141 Wooster Street
New York, NY 10012
www.overlookpress.com
For bulk and special sales, please contact sales@overlookny.com

LONDON:
Duckworth
90-93 Cowcross Street
London EC1M 6BF
www.ducknet.co.uk
info@duckworth-publishers.co.uk

Library of Congress Cataloging-in-Publication Data
Cebrián, Juan Luis, 1945–
[Pianista en el burdel. English]
The piano player in the brothel / Juan Luis Cebrian ;
introduction by Harold Evans.
p. cm.
Essays.
ISBN 978-1-59020-394-1
I. Evans, Harold, 1928– II. Title.
PQ6653.E27P5313 2011
864'.64—dc22
2010047283

A catalogue record for this book is available from the British Library

Typeformatting by Neuwirth & Associates

Printed in the United States
1 3 5 7 9 10 8 6 4 2

ISBN 978 1 59020 394 1 (US)
ISBN 978 0 7156 3977 1 (UK)

CONTENTS

"Don't tell my mother I'm a journalist. She thinks I play piano at the whorehouse."

Popular saying

INTRODUCTION

We take it for granted that Spain is a vibrant democracy. We should remember when it wasn't, when General Franco led a nationalist coup against the elected Republican government. Franco triumphed in the grisly civil war that followed and established himself as a dictator with the support of Fascist Germany and Italy. Franco was more of a hard-line conservative authoritarian than a Fascist, but he ran the country with an iron fist for thirty-six years, violently suppressing dissent and censoring the press. Gradually, in the exigencies of the cold war, a prospering Spain was welcomed back into the Western community of nations, and at the end of his life Franco redeemed himself in the eyes of many by arranging an orderly transition to rule by King Juan Carlos. The king at once instituted a parliamentary democracy and Spain lived happily ever after.

Not exactly. Only five years after Franco's death Spain's fledgling democracy was once more threatened by a military coup. The multitudes of visitors to Spain who feel the reverberations of history in Madrid and Barcelona and Granada and Cordoba, capital of the Islamic caliphate, probably haven't a clue about February 23, 1981, as relevant to Spain's history as any stone monument in a city square. A lieutenant colonel, one Antonio Tejero, burst into the elected Spanish Congress of Deputies supported by 200 armed officers. They sprayed the ceiling with a submachine–gun fire and informed the terrified deputies crouching on the floor that they were hostages pending the arrival of an official to acknowledge the colonel and his plotters as the new rulers of Spain. Tanks were on the streets in Valencia, by order of the captain general of the Third Military Region. Madrid's radio and TV station was seized by the plotters and duly announced their triumph. Spanish democracy was over again.

Well, not yet. Two important institutions stood between the plotters and a return to authoritarian rule for heaven knows how long this time: King Juan Carlos and the press. And by the press I mean preeminently *El País*, the newspaper edited by the author of this book, Juan Luis Cebrián. Early in the evening he got out a special edition of his paper. It reported what had happened and carried a biting condemnation on the illegality of the coup, a call to the country to stand by king, constitution, and democracy. They rushed copies to the king. A copy reached the Chamber where Tejero stood at the rostrum with his gun. One of the beleaguered deputies, Javier Solana, remembers breathing more easily when he looked up, astounded to see Tejero holding a copy of *El País*. Tejero might as well have been holding a grenade with the pin out; he was in effect reading his political obituary. His co-plotter, an insurgent general who was supposed to take firm control of television and radio, lost his nerve. About six hours after receiving the edition of *El País*, at 1:14 a.m. on February 24, the king in full military regalia was able to appear on national television and denounce the plotters.

The story of the coup that collapsed is as important in any history of the press as Watergate or the Pentagon Papers, but too little known outside Spain. In his new book Cebrián has chosen not to relate his heroic role, but it forms a backlight to his thoughtful essays on the press. His sketch of how news and comment were managed in a military dictatorship has a comic-opera quality it did not have in its heyday. Maybe even then, by comparison, say, with the way they went about these things in North Korea and Brezhnev's Russia, Spanish insouciance took some of the venom out of the sting, but it was certainly stultifying. Only the government could authorize a newspaper; publishers had to be licensed. "Apart from intellectual delirium," as Cebrián puts it, censorship worked like a bureaucratic machine.... Executive editors were appointed by the minister and everything published—news, photographs, advertising—had to pass official inspection. It was unthinkable, of course, that Franco could ever err. Cebrián describes how the orders came down to celebrate the glorious historic naval feats of Spain (passing lightly by those of 1588 and 1898, I imagine): "His idea of Spain satisfied a dictator whose empire consisted largely of cultural obscurantism and religious fanaticism." Cebrián was for a time part of the machinery as vice-director of Informaciones. He thought that with this grand title he could pass a long report saying that Franco's speech was "warmly received" without needing to punctuate Franco's words with "applause," "loud applause," "shouts of acclaim," "laughter," "wild applause," and a similar pepper pot of insertions by the censor. Cebrián's editing was regarded as akin to treason. "New evidence suggested my militant Marxism, although I have never been a militant for anything, except commonw sense."

The transition to democracy was awkward. Spain at all levels had only the vaguest notions of how the freedom the king ordained worked or was supposed to work, how the country could advance at all when ills could be ventilated, wielders of power held accountable, reputations assailed. The press, which had learned to live in authoritarian society but never lost its ideals, was the only institution really capable of teaching democracy to people who had never lived in a democracy. The trade unions had been forbidden, the judiciary and other social institutions were ineffectual, economic forces were weak, and the military leaders were confused. *El País* became a forum for debate and conciliation, a symbol of the transition, but Cebrián notes that its subsequent professional and commercial success "is still resented in certain circles." Cebrián is no mere booster. He is caustic about corruption of the ideals that animate responsible journalism. The perversion of investigative journalism, especially on Spanish television, he calls "a curse of our time." The *New York Times Magazine* revelations (9/3/2010) about how Rupert Murdoch's *News of the World* newspaper in Britain found a way into private voice-mail messages had not broken when Cebrián was writing furiously how some journalists had become spies and informers, gross invaders of privacy, smear artists in the vein of Joe McCarthy. It's not a Spanish custom. It is an international plague, manifest in particular in obnoxious websites that trade in abuse and paranoia, "their arbitrariness unchecked."

Cebrián's journalism is rooted in reason and history. His prodigious experience and dedication lends authority to the other issues he touches—terrorism, language, Hispanic America, the effect of media conglomeration, the future of journalism in the digital era. I got to know him when he visited the *Sunday Times* of London in the seventies before he launched *El País*, and ever since have admired how he and his colleagues created a new kind of newspaper: tabloid in format but the epitome of elegance and restraint in design, culturally sensitive, responsible and brave, rather like the man himself.

HAROLD EVANS, *September 2010*

THE PIANO
PLAYER IN
THE BROTHEL

THE MYTH OF WATERGATE

IN 1972 WASHINGTON police discovered a break-in at the headquarters of the Democratic Party. This apparently minor episode—a wiretapping operation—would lead to arguably the greatest confrontation between political power and the media in U.S. history. By the time the "episode" was over in August 1974, when President Nixon resigned, the name of this upscale office complex in the District of Columbia would be lodged not only in America's psyche, but also in the annals of journalism.

When Katharine Graham, who had inherited the *Washington Post* from her husband, was asked to call off her reporters from the investigation of White House involvement, the *Post*'s lawyers and managers repeatedly warned about the dangers of confronting the government: shareholder value and advertising revenue would decline, putting the company's television licenses at risk. Graham, who had faced a similar decision a year earlier with the Pentagon Papers, did not flinch. She resorted to capital markets for financial backing and lent her full support to her executive editor, Ben Bradlee, and his team.

A newspaper is a commercial enterprise, and as such it must further the interests of its owners and clients. Yet it is also a voice of the people. It must place its readers' interests before any other. Such was the prevailing philosophy at the time, one that made thousands of journalists throughout the world proud, if not always successful.

Watergate was a reminder of journalism's role as a watchdog against corruption and has come to symbolize journalistic independence, a check against political power. The idea of journalism as a "counterpower" emerged after Watergate, a theory formulated by then French president Valéry Giscard D'Estaing and subsequently taken up by political scientists. Yet I am not sure that today's media is anything more than an appendage of power, or perhaps power's afterglow.

An independent media is a myth, which is fine, perhaps necessary, as long as that myth doesn't become dogma, for the media occasionally shows contempt for individual rights and often acts in arbitrary ways. Journalism in general, and U.S. journalism in particular, has changed substantially since Watergate—from technological innovation to the structure of ownership.

Electronic media has forced newspapers to cut back on analysis and opinion while increasing the number of pages and color photos, first in advertising and later in content. Legendary newspapers, like the London *Times*, have transformed from top-quality publications with sober appearances—partly embodied in the paper's special texture—to merry outfits of sensationalism. Meanwhile, the evening edition has become an anachronism, a victim of television.

The digital media has brought about even more fragmentation as Internet readers increasingly seek to customize their news. Size has become necessary for survival. Family-owned newspapers have been gobbled up, and media companies now own leisure and entertainment units as part of their portfolios. Wall Street noticed all of this long ago; "going public" soon became the order of the day.

Today, the press's independence—so-called freedom of expression—has further been encroached upon by new realities and threats. The war against terrorism is among the most widely used clichés employed by governments to justify human rights violations. More recently, the economic crisis has inflamed the censoring zeal of thousands of bureaucrats throughout the world. Regulatory agencies in charge of overseeing capital markets seem more interested in limiting freedom of information than catching culprits of greed. Such is the case of the Comisión Nacional del Mercado de Valores (Spain's equivalent of the U.S. Securities and Exchange Commission). Absurdly, in lawmaking delirium, it pretends to punish rumor-mongers, an endeavor as commendable as it is futile: insidious debates ensue as to when a rumor becomes news or can be dismissed as gossip.

Bill Kovach and Tom Rosenstiel, founders of the Committee of Concerned Journalists, spent years talking to colleagues, readers, businessmen and women, advertisers, and ordinary citizens. They attempted to identify the essential elements of their profession—like fire, water, air, and earth for the ancients. Their conversations and experiences were gathered in the book *The Elements of Journalism*, in which they show how journalism, even on the Internet, still adheres to a few basic principles that not only identify it as a profession, but also demand a certain commitment from its practitioners:

Journalism's first obligation is to the truth.

Its first loyalty is to citizens.

Its essence is the discipline of verification.

Its practitioners must remain independent.

It must work as an independent monitor of power.

It must provide a forum for public criticism and compromise.

It must strive to make the significant interesting and relevant.

It must keep the news comprehensive and proportional.

Its practitioners must be allowed to exercise personal conscience.

It would be difficult to say more with fewer words. Of course these nine rules can easily be summarized, as with Moses and the Ten Commandments: journalism must be truthful and independent.

Truthfulness demands that journalists attempt to report events faithfully. Data should not be manipulated, nor doctored for convenience; verification must be strict, and journalists must be exhaustive in proof, plural in point of view, careful in nuance. Above all, they must acknowledge mistakes and be prepared to pay for them. Independence implies fulfilling the social role of journalism, not administering truth according to the pressures and conveniences of a politician, nor bearing witness for judges. Journalists must be critical, vigilant, and willing to engage, yet they must not let the passion for words smother the passion for truth.

Freedom of expression is essential in a thriving democracy, perhaps more so than political parties or parliamentary representation. Everyone knows this, yet selfish politicians have always hidden behind their office rather than honor the will of their constituents. Election as a blank check is unwarranted. Politicians must honor participatory democracy, must manifest the will of the people.

Nixonian arrogance must be avoided. We all know this and yet so many go astray.

I met the former president a year after the Watergate scandal broke, when one of his books was being published in Spain. He seemed bitter, resentful, and stubborn. He didn't seem to understand how his foreign policy achievements had been tarnished by his attempts to discredit his rivals. I also met Ben Bradlee over dinner one summer night in Paris. He was still youthful and happy at eighty years old, and teased us about disclosing the identity of "Deep Throat," the main source in the Watergate case, who died in late 2008. Someone commented on the personal lives of Woodward and Bernstein.

Bernstein had become something of a guru, giving lectures and writing books like *His Holiness*—a biography of Pope John Paul II (Karol Wojtyla)—which was recommended to me by Gabriel García Márquez, and which I strongly recommend to anyone interested in the Catholic Church's worldly power. Woodward continued working as a reporter after Watergate, apparently with the same enthusiasm and determination of his youth, which led him to become one of the most respected and feared journalists in his city. A few years ago Woodward and

Bernstein decided to sell their notes, recordings, and private documents from the Watergate investigation. They received $5 million.

The contribution of Watergate to the history of journalism has been very important, yet its mythical character can be problematic. Colleagues have become obsessed with forcing heads of state to resign, an obsession absent from the principles listed above. Such zealous pursuits seldom serve the public interest, and often leave newspapers and journalists looking provincial and marginal in the eyes of the international media. This has certainly been the case in Spain.

Perversion in investigative journalism, especially on television, is another curse. Journalists become spies, informers, or even thieves, indiscriminately—and sometimes abusively—invading the privacy of individuals, often in the name of free speech. Clandestine wiretappings, suggestions of wrongdoing, corruption before the fact, deceit and lies as a work method: such practices by "aggressive" journalists are often justified by the end result. Investigative journalism—requiring hard work, attention to detail, rigor, and time—should not be confused with hack journalism, whose practitioners are akin to police informers or political puppets in totalitarian societies.

Relations between politicians and journalists have always been strained, ever since Darius, king of Persia, killed the messenger announcing the defeat of his armies by the Greeks at Marathon (490 BCE). The truth irritates the prince when it contradicts his wishes or hinders his intentions. The history of journalism is full of conflicts with governments, courts, and other social institutions. Journalists often present themselves as martyrs and show us their wounds as evidence of their willingness to fight for freedom.

Thomas Jefferson famously said, "Were it left to me to decide whether we should have a government without newspapers or newspapers without a government, I should not hesitate a moment to prefer the latter." Jefferson made this statement while an ambassador in Paris. Once he was in power it didn't take long for him to censure the press for criticizing his government. Of course, this complicated relationship is not confined to politicians. Writers, intellectuals, and renowned journalists have praised the sublime functions of the press, only to disparage those same functions later on. Kierkegaard, the father of existentialism, complained bitterly, "Were it not for the press, I would dare trust my own forces: but it is awful that each week or each day a single man can have between 40,000 and 50,000 people saying and thinking the exact same thing. [...] Alas, poor press! If Jesus Christ were to return to earth—just as true as I am alive—his enemies would not be the Pharisees but the journalists."

Journalists have traditionally had poor relationships with political power in general, and are often viewed skeptically by those with dubious intentions. Indeed, Balzac once said, "If the press did not exist, it would be necessary not to invent it." The epigraph at the beginning of this chapter is a terrific illustration of the skepticism and suspicion with which journalists are regarded by traditional elements of society, although my favorite humorous quote about journalism comes from our Italian colleagues: "Working is even worse."

I've gone out of my way to describe the problematic position of the press because it is an essential factor, along with the struggle for freedom within nineteenth-century Romanticism, in the establishment of the press as the "fourth estate." This expression shadows us like a ghost. Unfortunately, like all such expressions, this one has some reality. Throughout the history of journalism, press barons have tried to influence—and sometimes even blackmail—readers, politicians, governments, and so on. It would be absurd to deny such power, even if it is only the power to influence, suggest, and condition. Yet it is not true power, since it lacks coercion and cannot impose its will. Some maintain that it is a de facto power with enormous capacity for destruction: it might not be able to put together a government, but it can overthrow one; it may not be able to consolidate a reputation, but its potential for slander and insult are almost unlimited.

In any case, newspapers, while still important, are losing relevance as social hierarchies break down and the Internet becomes even more prominent. Today, nobody believes that newspapers are more important than television during an election. Images have uncontested primacy over any other media in determining social behaviors, habits, tastes, fashion, values, and so on.

During the Second World War, radio emerged as an important medium, and its widespread application to stir hearts and minds was not confined to Nazism and Fascism. Churchill's speeches encouraging the British during the bombings are unforgettable, as are De Gaulle's harangues to the French Resistance. Freedom of expression was being rapidly transformed by citizens and leaders, and the latter were determined to use it for propaganda purposes. Yet freedom of the press, suggesting equality and choice, was taken for granted in democratic societies just as much as the principles of separation of powers and universal suffrage.

Now we must seek new ways to protect the freedom of the press, since the threats of censorship are no longer limited to external pressure, but essentially arise from the very organization and behavior of the Internet. These are the issues addressed in this book. I have tried to avoid lecturing. Instead, I've attempted to share my experience with the hope that a new generation of journalists finds it useful. The best way to transform the world is to help others understand it. This is the calling of journalism.

Watergate can help us understand the importance of modesty with respect to our difficult task, the importance of distance from power, of stepping down from the balconies and platforms on which power is celebrated. The importance of the *Washington Post* with respect to the political history of the world lies above all in the insight and professional perseverance of journalists devoted to sources on the ground and contacts at the Washington police department. Nurturing these contacts is the first obligation of any journalist. Everything else—the grand philosophies, the halos of importance and reverence, the vanity of success, and the pretentiousness of thought—comes afterward, preceded by a short and laconic police note.

HACKS, GEESE, AND TRICKSTERS

WHILE SEARCHING THROUGH my library one day, I found a strange book of outrageous newspaper headlines and articles, the kind of book published every now and then to illustrate the ignorance, vulgarity, or simple haste of those in charge of getting out a newspaper. On the book's cover was the first page of a local Spanish newspaper. The headline read: "Crushed to Death by a Rock While Making Love to a Chicken."

Next to the headline a low-resolution photograph offered irrefutable proof of the event, in which a boulder weighing several tons had crushed a poor peasant enjoying the hen's company. One might think that such a story is an atypical view of journalism, yet ever since the Venetian *gazzettanti* and the Parisian *canards*, outrageous news has enjoyed an admirable degree of attention.

During the seventeenth century, in exchange for a *gazzetta*, the Venetian Republic's smallest coin, the gondoliers would sell a pamphlet consisting of several manuscript sheets mixing facts and lies, important and bizarre events, slander and denunciation, slurs and reports that traders brought to the city. The news would be transmitted by word of mouth among merchants, sailors, and longshoremen.

The Parisian *canard*'s etymology relates to jargon used by peddlers of gossip and rumors; it was also a pamphlet of half-truths and full lies. Many of these stories were nonsense, but people liked them and were willing to pay, just as if they were having their palm read. Given a choice, we prefer imaginary stories over truthful stories. We find the former less disturbing.

Governments soon discovered the propaganda potential of gazettes, and kings and court favorites promptly granted publishing rights to certain subjects. The word *gazette* was sanctified and universalized, no longer a coin but a printed

newspaper. However, in Spain we still using the term
gacetillero (gazette writer) to refer to hack journalists.

Journalism has combined the high and the low
throughout history. Columnists and reporters never cease
to claim modest pedigree while aspiring to patronage. As
permanent palace residents, we are viewed as necessary
intruders, particularly since kings and nobility are now
elected. Our strength comes from our populism: the
tricks and ploys of the Venetian *gazzettanti* or the breed-
ers of the Parisian *canards*—real geese whose honks ech-
oed through the slums—are not new to us.

The spirit of our profession can trace its roots to Roman
mythology, to Mercury. Mercury, like his predecessor
Hermes, was the Roman god of commerce and the patron
of traders and robbers. He was also, particularly in his
Greek incarnation, the messenger of the gods and the
protector of eloquence, traits that quickly turned him
into the patron of liars and an accomplice of swindlers.

The first journalistic "mercuries" were established in
Belgium and France in the mid-seventeenth century. In
1827, Pedro Félix de Vicuña —along with two typogra-
phers, Tomás G. Wells, from the United States, and Igna-
cio Silva Medina—founded *El Mercurio de Valparaíso*, the

direct predecessor of Chile's *El Mercurio*, later bought by Agustín Edwards in 1880. Today it is the oldest Spanish-language newspaper in the world, although *Gaceta de Madrid*, the Spanish official state gazette, was founded in 1661 and played an important role during the political conspiracies of the eighteenth century. However, it is now dedicated to publishing laws, decrees, and regulations. In January 2009, the government decided to publish it exclusively online.

However it is considered, modern journalism is linked to money and power. It also remains close to literature and, although not mentioned as often, to coffee and tobacco, sublime drugs glorified by civilization. Bologna's *Il Resto del Carlino* might be the most sophisticated masthead in Italy. Like the gazettes mentioned above, its name alludes, in a very refined manner, to the coin used to buy it. The newspaper's price was related to that of the popular Tuscan cigars smoked in the cafés and saloons of the era. A cigar cost eight cents, and the buyer would normally pay with a ten-cent coin, popularly known as a "carlino" in the Bologna area, so the tobacconist would return two cents in change.

Some smart publisher from Florence decided to publish

a newspaper under the title *Il Resto del Sigaro* (literally, the cigar's change), fixing its price at two cents. The Bologna printers imitated the name but decided to name their newspaper *Il Resto del Carlino* (the carlino's change) to give it a local identity. For ten cents one could smoke a Tuscan cigar and read an eight-page daily newspaper while sitting comfortably in any of the city's cafés, commenting on the news, exchanging opinions, and hatching political and literary conspiracies. This was also the routine at the café that Benjamin Harris established in Boston in 1868.

An English bookseller, Harris had gone to Boston to escape the political repression in London, where he faced a 5,000-pound fine for distributing subversive pamphlets. In addition to his café, he also founded a bookstore and started a periodical devoted to current news and commentary. *Publick Occurrences, Both Foreign and Domestick* was the title of the three-page newspaper, published without official permission and immediately closed after its first edition. Bernard A. Weisberger, a historian of U.S. journalism, sees Harris as the "prototype of the American journalist—active, aggressive and independent."

So-called responsible journalism was exemplified by the Scottish-born John Campbell, a post office employee who founded the *Boston News-Letter* in 1704, which was published with all the necessary official permits. Since then, "responsibility" has frequently been seen as submission, or the agreement to disseminate whatever is deemed suitable by the authorities. Some saw Campbell's acquiescence as political correctness, which often entails submission to power. It's a paradox: newspapers attack the establishment, yet often grovel to it.

Journalism in its infancy was more concerned with price than credibility, and the respect that publications garnered derived not from truthfulness but from their relationship with the king. They had to flatter and entertain with their stories. Some subjects were interesting, squalid, and grisly, others cheerful, yet all of them featured either a deep human touch or extreme political activism. They were masters at combining pleasure and conspiracy, defending such values as freedom and liberty while simultaneously producing abundant profits. Such combinations of the high and the low have never abated. Newspapers are microcosms of society: news and opinions, coups and scientific discoveries, reports of moral decadence involving chickens, even warnings of death by stoning because of bestiality.

There is an English saying that anyone walking down the street who sees what's happening and tells about it is a journalist; a Spanish proverb states that "nothing is true or false, everything depends on the color of the lens through which we look." Our readers' attentions depend greatly on how we tell stories, what is emphasized, the kind of adjectives we employ, how transparent and objective we are.

Someone once told the story of an aspiring journalist sent by the editor in chief to a nearby store to fetch cigarettes and matches. When the aspiring journalist returned, the editor in chief threw the tobacco in the trash and said, "Now tell me, what did you see while running your errand?"

Although observation is essential to journalism, it is not exclusive to journalists. Spies, policemen, and novelists pay more attention to anecdotes than we do. For centuries journalism has been accused of poetic license, perhaps in the willful distortion of reality, the reinterpretation of facts according to the journalist's editor, or simply incompetence and malevolence.

Journalism has always had close ties to show business and entertainment as well, in addition to other elements of Romanticism and patriotism; this was especially the case in the nineteenth century. The introduction of one-cent dailies in the United States and the invention of the rotary press fueled the popularity of newspapers. Sales rose from about 8,000–10,000 copies on average to more than 100,000 copies. The Parisian geese turned into migratory flocks that aroused the passions of politicians and the people.

Spain's colonial war of the nineteenth century, which resulted in the loss of Cuba, Puerto Rico, and the Philippines, was primarily promoted in the columns of Hearst's newspapers in the United States, which had no qualms about manipulating and lying, extolling the patriotic spirit of Americans in their solidarity with the rebels from the Caribbean Pearl. Citizen Kane's methods, an early marriage of capitalism to journalism, were not much different from those employed decades earlier by Karl Marx and the *New Gazette of the Rhine*.

"The charter that governed the editorial office," said Friedrich Engels, "was simply Marx's will. A great daily newspaper that must be printed by a fixed deadline cannot consistently defend its points of view under any other regime." The truth is that democracy was already rare in editorial offices. From the *Gazette*, Marx stoked the flames of German revolution and war with Russia. Just as with Hearst's employees, Marx's journalists were not only editors but also fighters. The newspaper's headquarters kept on hand eight rifles, 250 rounds of ammunition, and Phrygian caps for all of its workers. The remarkable difference between these two journalistic enterprises is that Hearst's empire still endures, while the gazette from the Rhine barely survived its first year. Lenin learned from Marx's mistake. He understood, with the publication of *Iskra*, that newspapers were the best agitators and organizers.

The history of journalism is intimately linked to the history of wars and revolutions, yet journalism has shown little interest in understanding their causes. Mass movements were once journalism's specialty, since newspapers addressed the masses. Journalists have always known that life and death, sex and love, blood and guts inspire humanity the most, irrespective of race, belief, or social status. In his brilliant book on Camus, Jean Daniel, founder of *Le Nouvel Observateur*, recounts what Sartre said at the beginning of their adventure: "Don't hesitate to talk about blood and sex. It's what the bourgeois like, and it provokes their feelings of guilt."

By the time Orson Welles's "War of the Worlds" premiered at the RKO New York Radio studios, there was enough professional expertise to produce news reports in the style of the great Shakespearean dramas or Hollywood scripts. Therefore, some listeners who tuned in halfway into the program believed they were hearing about a real extraterrestrial invasion; some jumped out the window in panic. Such behavior was not uncommon among Americans during that time, especially during the Great Depression. Thankfully, this behavior of jumping off one's balcony in a panic has largely disappeared, although newspaper publishers continue devising new methods to provoke their readers.

Welles proved how easily the mass media could manipulate reality and confuse it with fiction, mix truth with lies; after all, as discussed above, journalism and show business were already in bed together. The emergence of radio, and television later on, had unforeseeable political consequences. Those in power discovered that, as it was in the days of princes and kings, intervention was necessary, this time in the guise of new permits and licenses required for citizens to exercise free speech.

Due to the narrowness of the radio-electric spectrum, or perhaps as a pretext, channel and frequency licensing was established to limit radio and television operations. It is as if modern bureaucrats had resurrected the royal decree of grants awarded for printing newspapers. Many governments who boast of their democratic credentials continue to license in the very same way today, rewarding friends and punishing enemies.

At the 1939 World's Fair in New York, NBC broadcast an address from President Roosevelt via 150 television sets displayed throughout the city. Soon, baseball games and boxing matches were televised. From the start, sports represented one of the most powerful engines driving growth in the world of communication. Along with pornography, it remains among the strongest stimuli for the development of advanced technology. My point with all this history is partly to show that those traits exhibited in the early days of journalism are still prevalent: on one side of the screen is a politician, on the other side entertainment.

The emergence of electronic media provoked a great deal of alarm among newspaper journalists and businessmen. Newspapers struggled to find a new role while trying to preserve their symbolic status. They improved their printing and distribution systems, incorporated photographs and, later on, color images, and kept relatively moderate prices. More important, they began to "explain" the news and disseminate their own opinions. They were proclaimed the champions of pluralism in comparison to one-trick television—which remained a private or public monopoly for a long time in many countries. Newspapers experimented with new journalistic formulas that produced such spectacular writers as Truman Capote and Gabriel García Márquez. They launched investigative journalism, which would eventually provoke President Nixon's wrath. Despite adversities, including the fact that 80 percent of the developed world received their news from the television as early as the 1960s, it became clear that all media was complementary and there was no reason to panic. Everyone had their place in the sun, including newspapers.

During the Victorian era, English newspapers financed costly expeditions to Africa, usually with geographical and historical societies; war correspondents also became common in the middle of the nineteenth century. The invention of new communication and transportation technologies promoted the reckless aspects of the trade and also created new specialties within journalism. A journalist could send telegrams, write obituaries at the editorial office, or parachute into a war-torn country armed only with a camera and a pen. Yet journalism's dualistic nature remained constant: the Court scribes freelanced—or perhaps more accurately, smart plebeians meddled in the corridors of power.

By the late 1970s and early 1980s, the printing and distribution revolution had begun. Daily newspapers gradually abandoned lead printing for electronic publishing. Processes that had revolutionized the press and had proven useful for more than a century, like the Linotype machine, were rendered obsolete in less than a decade. Large newspapers continued to be vital, but they were no longer the prime movers and shakers. The development of satellites allowed them to expand coverage into local markets. The press had always been a local phenomenon at heart, or only a national one in small and average-sized states.

Due to its importance in shaping public opinion, as well as creating and maintaining collective identities, newspaper distribution has received generous public support in many countries. Subsidized postal rates and even special trains or airplanes are often arranged to distribute what is considered a necessity in every country, under all types of political systems: democracies, where the news is based on public opinion, and dictatorships, where it is manipulated and turned into propaganda. Satellites have proven useful not only for delivering television content to cable networks, but also for printing off-site and enabling quick delivery across the globe. As a result of these developments, the *Wall Street Journal*, a relatively small newspaper, now produces the largest print run in the United States, and the *Herald Tribune* has become a truly global newspaper, published on five continents.

Television followed a similar path, and the Moscow Olympic Games of 1980 marked CNN's emergence as the first global news network. A few years later, their coverage of the Gulf War ensured CNN's role as a primary source of information during world crises. And when the United States and the United Kingdom decided to invade Iraq—with the support of the shamefully mismanaged government in Madrid—we were offered a glimpse of how live television coverage around the world could change the strategy and meaning of a war. The Iraq War was described with unparalleled detail and starkness. Hundreds of journalists reported the story, as winners and as losers. Indeed, it might even be said that negative European public opinion and reaction to the United States' execution of the war was based on the suffering endured by war correspondents. More than twenty were killed in a war that should never have happened.

In 1993, the U.S. government promoted a liberalization of telecommunications by opening up intelligence, defense, and research networks. When Bill Clinton took office, a few hundred Web pages existed on the Internet. Today they number in the billions. Hypertext language was created in 1989, and the first Web browsers did not reach the market until the early 1990s. In less than two decades the growth of general Internet use has been explosive, and its development has been achieved at a remarkable pace.

The eventual burst of the dot-com stock market bubble stunned the public, and some thought that the Internet's impact had been exaggerated. Yet, the current financial disaster, which has been defined as the first global economic crisis, is directly related to the global implementation of digital systems. The digital revolution, with the Internet as its main paradigm, is real and, like all revolutions, is having profound effects on society. As with all technological leaps, the speed at which it proceeded can best be appreciated with hindsight. Only then are we able to see how fast the leaps occurred.

Much of the available information in the world is now on the Internet, accessible to anyone connected to the system and able to use it. No longer valid is the saying, "He who has the information has the power." The old dream of a universal library continues, as knowledge is collected, classified, and filed, readily available to all and at all times. In many ways, it is a special kind of knowledge: dynamic, interactive, dialectic, and expansive.

Perhaps the former president of Spain, Felipe González, said it best: "We are unable to understand that information by itself is no longer power; power consists of the reasonable management and coordination of information to attain operative results. Leadership is not proved by having information but by the ability to produce it and use it."

Such an environment must necessarily influence journalism. That information is no longer power is due to the plethora of data and news, to the relentless offerings of newspapers, radio stations, television, and the Internet. More information does not mean better information, and here is where journalism's new role might be found: as a mediator for society and individuals—selecting, analyzing, and explaining information, as well as discovering publicly available information that nobody knows how to access.

In a way, we are going back in time. The Parisian *canard* and the Venetian *menanti* or *gazzettanti* were able to do as they pleased. On the Internet, news gets mixed with rumors, deception, and fantasies all the time, and it is sold for less than the *gazzetta*—it is free. The final step in the analogy is the search for benefactors. Like Horace, the Internet aspires to the emperor's sponsorship, even if the emperor looks like a bottle of Coca-Cola.

Moreover, the Internet allows a single journalist to produce a newspaper and to target it to single readers, as in times of old when a single man with a fountain pen and a stack of paper sheets could take on the world. This is how the *New York Herald* was founded by James Gordon Bennett in 1835. He worked as reporter, director, typographer, printer, advertising agent, and marketing expert.

Some people anguish about the future of newspapers (and bound books), which Bill Gates predicted several years ago would survive for only a few years. Of course such predictions are rash, considering technological innovation, environmental concerns, economics, and, most important, consumer habits and social infrastructures. Yet, we must not fear innovation. Is it not better to read a flexible, well-lit liquid crystal screen with large letters and hypertext capability than an old, poorly printed newspaper full of imperfections? Contrary to McLuhan, the basic issue is not the medium but the message.

An online newspaper is no longer a periodical, since it is not published periodically, but rather updated continuously. Text, video, and audio are converging in new technologies. A global market has emerged wherein millions of individuals can be reached irrespective of time and place. The poet Paul Valéry once said that the future isn't what it used to be. Each day we seem to wake up to an unknown and surprising world, where everything must be built from the ground up.

Many of us felt this way about the attacks of September 11, 2001, witnessed live on television by hundreds of millions of people. It was a surreal drama that seemed to come from a Hollywood script, the difference being that the victims were as real as those in Afghanistan, Iraq, or the metro stations in Madrid and London. Is there any better metaphor for the globalization of information, the economy, power, war and peace, terrorism and fear, than September 11 and subsequent events?

But what should journalists do in a world flooded by images and propaganda? Some worry, rightfully, about authoritarian trends in the world's oldest democracies, where citizens are inhibited and frightened by the devious and insidious threat of terrorism. Increasingly, one hears protests against self-censorship, or outright censorship, in the Western media. We face a difficult choice between security and freedom—always a balancing act in any democracy.

The scale seems to be tipping in favor of security. It was striking to compare the treatment of September 11 attacks by American networks and Arab Al Jazeera television. American networks scrupulously avoided televising the images of lifeless bodies. During the wars in Afghanistan and Iraq, as well as during the Christmas 2008 crisis in Gaza, Al Jazeera constantly broadcast the suffering of children and elders. Viewers were bombarded daily with images of mutilated bodies. Where is the subtle line that separates propaganda from the duty of providing information? As much as the excesses committed by the United

States can and should be criticized, I cannot but praise the responsibility shown by its media during September 11. On the other hand, I protested and still protest the blatant manipulation of viewers with respect to the coverage of the Iraq War by the large television networks. In Spain, the victims of terrorism are constantly used to raise public support of controversial policies. This is a delicate issue, and it is easy to generalize. My intent here, in this book, is not to criticize but rather to reflect and question.

FREEDOM FOR GOOD DEEDS

I STARTED WORKING as a professional journalist in the summer of 1962, taking advantage of an internship offered by the Official School of Journalism. I chose to work at *Pueblo*, an evening daily connected to Franco's trade unions, at the time directed by Emilio Romero. Even those opposed to Franco's regime acknowledged Romero's abilities as a promoter of debate. Everyone took note whenever he published one of his famous "roosters," which is what he called his articles. The image of a rooster always accompanied the title, perhaps an exercise in arrogance (we weren't yet acquainted with Kentucky Fried Chicken's famous Colonel), as it seemed to imply that he was cock of the walk, king of the coop.

When I entered the editorial office on the first day of my internship, the first thing I saw was a heavy typewriter flying across the room. The newspaper's movie critic had thrown it at the municipal chronicler, who luckily dodged it. Evidently, the municipal chronicler had made a tasteless remark about the newspaper's executive editor. I quickly understood two things: the executive editor was controversial, and one risked being crushed by an Underwood typewriter if one questioned the editor's merits.

As I said, it was 1962, and Emilio Romero was already the most important journalist under Franco's regime. Only the myth surrounding Manuel Aznar Zubigaray—the grandfather of the future president of Spain under the Popular Party—could compete with him. The difference lay in the fact that Manuel Aznar used journalism as a springboard to politics, while Romero lived and died a journalist, perhaps because he knew that the regime's apparatchiks would never offer a government position to a plebeian.

Romero's journalistic contributions were aided greatly by his invaluable editor in chief, Jesús de la Serna. He opened up the newspaper to the new generations, promoted street journalism, and got interested in technological innovation. He also facilitated a certain "controlled dissidence" that helped identify his newspaper as the voice of the proletariat within the regime, a faction that deserved no credit in the eyes of the opposition, but distressed the Catholic right wing.

I worked for him for six years. Despite the differences in our politics and our ages, he named me editor in chief of the local pages, where both the municipal chronicler and the aggressive critic had once worked.

Later, for a period of a few short months, he put me in charge of the Third Page, where members of the clandestine Communist Party, post-council priests like Juan Arias, rebel actors like Marsillach, and a few other regime opponents were allowed to voice their opinions—as long as their articles were deemed acceptable by the authorities. Emilio Romero had a reputation for being authoritarian and egocentric, as well nepotistic. But he left me alone and defended me against the reactionary elements of the regime.

In contrast to the servile attitude of many of his collaborators, I realized that his immense vanity was more disposed to dialectics than submission. He hardly traveled out of Spain because, among other reasons, he was averse to flying and couldn't learn foreign languages He represented a traditionalist intellectual movement that included popular columnists like Francisco Umbral and which was much appreciated by our country's right wing.

Emilio was a terrifying writer, with arrogant prose and sharp judgment, good for newspapers, but not so much for literature. He benefited from the protection of Minister Solís, the smiling face of Franco's regime; enjoyed Juan Domingo Perón's friendship; mingled with intellectuals returning from exile; and struggled to find a role for himself and his newspaper among socialites and actors (he wrote a handful of mediocre theater reviews).

Marquises, soccer players, ambassadors, bullfighters, flamenco dancers, trendy actresses, bankers, *poètes maudits*, and paparazzi reporters all sought his friendship and influence. He was generous to all, though occasionally vindictive toward a few. He turned *Pueblo* into a factory of new journalists and served as a role model for many young professionals dazzled by his aura. But the aura began to fade as Franco faded. We discovered that the myth of Emilio Romero, like so many other myths of his time, was nothing more than fiction.

To be fair, Romero didn't have much room to operate. The press was governed by an emergency law passed during the Civil War, in April 1938. Its first article declared: "The institution of the periodical press will be organized, supervised, and controlled by the State." Irrespective of one's political stripes, irrespective of one's popularity, nothing could be said that wasn't convenient to those in power. The Press Law of 1938 was originally provisional, according to its authors, but it was not an improvisation. It fit with the totalitarian spirit of the rebels who rose up in arms against the republic and their Fascist vision for society, which the Church soon joined by creating what was termed National-Catholicism, the backbone of the dictatorship. The decree's preamble stated:

Today we can truly and solemnly declare freedom of the press. A freedom that is made of rights and duties, one that will never again lead to that democratic decadence that has questioned and threatened our homeland and State, and proclaimed the right to publish lies, deceit, and

defamation as the method for the destruction of Spain
that has been decided by the hostility of secret powers.

The apostles of this new homeland set up a complex bureaucracy geared toward organizing, supervising, and controlling the press. Government employees toiled enthusiastically at this task, first in the Ministry of the Interior, later in the Ministry of Education, and finally, starting in 1951, in the Ministry of Information and Tourism. Censoring organisms multiplied, and consignment was frequently employed. This procedure not only allowed censors to avoid the publication of inconvenient news, but also guaranteed that their leadership strategy was properly communicated to the public. A note from August 1946 read: "In order to prepare the public for the government's upcoming decisions on prices and the reduction of the cost of living, your newspaper must publish an editorial that will generally refer to the relevance of this issue to our nation in the terms I hereby transcribe." The sender would offer a series of headlines and slogans to be used by the editorial writer, one of which I find irresistible: "A high cost of living stimulates the mean ambitions of the greedy."

Newspaper directors had obvious reasons to heed such instructions, since they were appointed by the government rather than by newspaper owners. This law, which applied to both private and public companies, was accepted by newspapers of great tradition and lineage, and was not abolished until the mid-1960s. Such was the stale atmosphere of Spanish journalism when I arrived at the editorial offices of *Pueblo*.

At the time, Gabriel Arias-Salgado directed the Ministry of Information and Tourism. He was a vivid reincarnation of Torquemada, the prominent leader of the Spanish Inquisition, whose stern character was inflamed by an authoritarian and fanatical nature; his name became a sort of trademark for Spanish obscurantism. He is the alleged author of the famous sentence, "All the freedom for truth, none for errors," which I have been unable to document. However, Gabriel Arias-Salgado's former boss, José Ibáñez Martín, who was minister of education during the 1940s, made a similar assertion and often declared shamelessly: "The sole purpose of true freedom is to serve the truth." Of course, it was the authorities who defined the good and the true.

A dictatorship's paternalistic side is often overlooked

amid its cruelty. Clearly, censorship and consignment existed in order to keep our mouths shut and promote political indoctrination. Yet many well-meaning bureaucrats also attempted to provide citizens and journalists with moral and ethical guidance—to save souls, as exemplified by the commentary about the cost of living.

Even in 1965, a note from Manuel Fraga's department (Ministry of Information and Tourism) warned that "within the realm of sports news, the principles of professional ethics require that information also be treated in a sportsmanlike fashion [...] a great effort must be made to calm passions, not to inflame them." This note, which I took from an excellent study by Manuel Fernández Areal ("The Evolution of the Concept of Freedom of the Press from the June 1938 Law until the Constitution of 1978") echoes another note from a decade earlier stating that coverage of soccer games should be limited to the actual match; any events not directly connected to the game should be ignored. Even idioms that might present controversy were forbidden, such as "treacherous tackle or dirty play, and in general anything that might worsen or exacerbate the passion among different Spanish regions."

The professional zeal and passion with which censors

performed their jobs had considerable effects on both grammar and vocabulary. On one occasion, Arias-Salgado's department sent a "compulsory insertion note, in bold characters on the front page," noting Franco's arrival to a town in Spain. The note mentioned how the church bells were tolling with joy. The bureaucrat in charge was informed that church bells ring in joy and toll only in mourning. The bureaucrat stood his ground, and the note was published the next day. The anecdote prompted poets to write a few verses that became famous in the oral history of Spanish journalism:

> Tolling bells are a somber sound,
> But they may be full of optimism,
> If ordered by the Ministry
> Of Information and Tourism.

Apart from the occasional intellectual delirium, censorship worked like a bureaucratic machine. Newspapers' preliminary government authorization, their executive editors, were appointed by the minister, and everything published—news, photographs, advertising—had to pass official inspection.

Editorial offices had a figure known as the "censorship liaison." His job consisted of checking proofs and filing them away for months and even years back as irrefutable evidence absolving newspaper publishers of responsibility—despite the fact that publishers were censors themselves under the "delegated censorship" system.

Since *Pueblo* was an evening newspaper, the entire inspection process—which involved the Ministry of Information contacting the Ministry of Foreign Affairs for diplomatic issues, or the military departments for defense matters—typically continued well into the evening. Our liaison would try to speed up the procedure, so the office could close for the night, by getting on the telephone to gather instructions. The instructions were often contradictory, and the censor had the right to change them at will, especially if one of his superiors voiced a different opinion.

The boldest editors in chief would challenge significant editorial decisions, sometimes successfully, resulting in many proofs covered with red ink and crowned with a purple or crimson stamp that read "authorized." This habit of using red ink for censoring originated centuries ago. The library at the Universidad de Salamanca has several works censored by the Inquisition; the offending paragraphs had been mutilated with blood-colored ink.

Manuel Fraga and the Ministry of Information and Tourism introduced a law in 1966 that seemed to be a blessing for journalists. The law did not introduce freedoms, nor did it eliminate censorship, but it removed the awkward procedure of sending galleys to the government for inspection every day. After all, a newspaper couldn't exist without the ministry's permission, which was often refused, and publishers were required to have a license. Such requirements prevented dissidents from reaching executive positions in newspapers. Hence, newspaper publishers, who received numerous threats proportionate to their professional responsibilities, simultaneously became the champions of freedom and its permanent repressors.

They struggled to publish news and opinions critical of the government. At the same time they had to practice self-censorship because they were subject to the sometimes unbearable pressure of the authorities. The head of state and the head of government could not be criticized, nor the army or its commanders; the unity of Spain could not be questioned, and Catholic morals must be observed and upheld at all times; strikes continued to be treated as an act of sedition. The press thus focused on municipal criticism, which the regime seemed to tolerate as long as it did not extend beyond dirty streets or zoning regulations (although a selected few continued to profit from changes in zoning laws and land use).

Along with the aforementioned prohibitions, circumstantial restrictions were issued periodically and faithfully transmitted to newspaper publishers by government employees. When a cholera outbreak hit several areas of Spain during the summer of 1972, the government decided to censor the news. It didn't want citizens to become alarmed; it was also worried about tourism.

The leniency or severity with which the ministry dealt with the infringement of rules was inversely proportional to how often infringement occurred. Books were censored less often than monthly publications, which were censored less often than weekly magazines, which in turn enjoyed more freedom than daily newspapers. The success of some publications of that period—*Cuadernos para el diálogo, Destino, Cambio 16,* and *Triunfo*—was largely due to censorship of the daily press, but also because companies that published daily newspapers were committed, in one way or another, to the system's survival.

But then a novel method of editorial corruption emerged: "editorial advertising." Newspapers published reports, articles, and information of interest to the government using a more formal method of consignment. Sometimes the authorities would send the material to the editorial offices, and in other instances the companies would send a collection of newspaper clips to the authorities as proof of their collaboration.

These special-interest articles increased and became more diverse as Franco's regime aged. There was editorial advertising on orange tree diseases, the African swine fever, but also pieces devoted to John of Austria and the role of Spain at the battle of Lepanto. In this last instance, Admiral Carrero Blanco was determined to inform the world about the naval feats of our ancestors. This idea of Spain satisfied a dictator whose empire consisted largely of cultural obscurantism and religious fanaticism.

Like many dictators, Franco was sheltered from criticism and surrounded by flattery. While visiting a province at the end of his dictatorship, severely ill, Franco's dull speech was interspersed with parenthetical statements in the press that supposedly reflected the crowd's enthusiasm: "(Applause, a big round of applause, a standing ovation, a voice that says: 'we owe it to you,' 'Franco, Franco, Franco!')." I thought, as the vice-director of Informaciones, that such interjections could be eliminated, at least in part, since an upcoming law on political associations was already being discussed and the dictator's death was presumably very close. I published the telegram without the flattering interruptions, and simply stated that Franco had received a warm round of applause at the end of his speech.

My boss, and my eternal mentor, Jesús de la Serna, whom I first met at the editorial office of *Pueblo*, was threatened by the minister with severe disciplinary measures and warned never to make such a blunder again. I was accused of censorship and of performing a sectarian manipulation of the objective information I had received from Efe, the government's press agency. New evidence suggested my militant Marxism played a part, although I have never been a militant of anything, except for common sense.

However, it must be acknowledged that Fraga's law regarding inspection represented a step in the right direction. Amid obstacles and persecutions, the press was the single forum for debate during the last years of the dictatorship. And it sure wasn't a free ride. The attorney general of the Supreme Court, Fernando Herrero Tejedor, said that, during 1967, the law's first year in effect, thirty-six disciplinary actions had been taken for violations of the Law of Press and Printing. Fourteen such cases were heard by the Public Order Court, consisting of judges specializing in political repression. Attorney General Herrero considered these figures to be very satisfactory, since they proved that journalists were being held accountable for their freedoms.

Though the attorney general was satisfied, fourteen political trials seemed too few for many other members of government. There were also dozens of administrative penalties, some involving substantial fines. The government issued reform article 165 of the Criminal Code, which included severe penalties for press infractions; later the Law of Official Secrets was enacted, which dealt a severe blow to Fraga's more or less liberalizing measures.

Soon student unrest erupted and the repressive machine revved up again. In 1968 the daily newspaper *Madrid* was suspended for four months for an article it published by Professor Calvo Serrer praising General De

Gaulle's voluntary retirement, a decision not shared by General Franco. Several books and periodicals were provisionally confiscated (*Cuadernos para el diálogo*, *Mundo*, *Sábado gráfico*, *Indice*, *Criterio*, the HOAC bulletin, and Pamplona's daily newspapers), and 266 administrative proceedings were opened against journalists and publishing companies. Néstor Luján, executive editor of *Destino*, was sentenced to eight months in prison and fined 10,000 peseta for publishing a letter attacking the use of Catalonian language, a charge that couldn't be taken seriously because *Destino* had a strong liberal record and had previously defended Catalonia's identity.

Despite this series of absurdities and persecutions, climaxing in the suspension of *Madrid*, Fraga's law marked the apex of censorship under Franco's regime. And it created a fracture in the dictatorship's sclerotic structure from which journalists and politicians profited. Freedom of the press was still tenuous, but it encouraged bold, or imprudent, journalists to begin to criticize the status quo. Hence, the press became a sort of a paper parliament, replacing an inane assembly whose members were appointed by the regime and who obediently indulged its desires for self-satisfaction.

The press was supposed to undergo a series of reforms planned by the dictatorship's more progressive elements. But Franco and Carrero Blanco halted many reforms, forbade many political associations, and boycotted another law on trade union liberty. Using the Law of Jurisdiction, military courts prosecuted more journalists, several of whom were court-martialed. In its repressive escalation against the press—which was then referred to as *canallesca*, or scoundrel—the government instituted an antiterrorist law that curtailed public liberties even more, including freedom of expression, under the pretext of fighting the growing violence of the Basque separatist movement. Once again, the fight against terrorism was used as an excuse for curtailing human rights. Franco's death was only four months away.

FROM TRANSITION TO THE RACK

MUCH HAS BEEN said and written about
the role of the press in creating political change. It would
be fair to acknowledge certain daily newspapers as leaders in democratic movements (a role often demanded by
readers), yet such expectations in Spain were unreasonable at the time. *El País* became a symbol of the transition
itself, and its subsequent professional and commercial
success is still resented in certain circles. On the other
hand, the pride and arrogance of a few who have contrib-
uted to that success is inexcusable. Certainly it is true that
political debate during the last ten years of the dictatorship

occurred only because of the press, particularly weekly and monthly publications. Newspapers provided a forum for debate and a stage for conciliation, particularly since political parties and trade unions were forbidden, social institutions remained ineffectual, economic forces were weak, and confusion reigned among military leaders.

The political debate would not have been possible had the "agreed rupture" in Franco's dictatorship not occurred. Franco's prohibitive laws remained in effect, but change was in the air, as they say. Yet the rupture wasn't a well-defined break; it was not revolutionary. Rather, it was an agreement that gradually enabled the press to perform its critical role during the early stages of the new regime— much to the chagrin and despair of those who hoped for a Francoist monarchy.

In a sense, newspapers performed a didactic function in that they had to teach democracy to people who had never lived in a democracy. Paradoxically, some newspapers and journals that had shown a strong commitment to freedom and opposed the dictatorship in its later years were swept away by the overwhelming commercial strength of many newer publications. Such was the case for *Cuadernos para el diálogo* and *Triunfo*, the memories of which should be preserved as an example for future generations.

Around 1976, the social leadership of newspapers and the enthusiasm of their readers led to what could be considered the golden age of Spanish journalism in the twentieth century. Journalists had become professionalized, despite the frequent skirmishes over licenses and requirements still necessary to practice journalism. Real intellectuals filled newspaper pages once again, printing plants were modernized, corruption in editorial offices and businesses was eliminated, and the independent character of public opinion was acknowledged. This road toward freedom of the press was full of contradictions, sacrifices, and difficulties, some of which were severe, but in the end, the results, until the late 1980s, could not have been better.

However, not all the relationships between journalists and politicians were pure, especially during the early days of the transition. Many misunderstandings occurred in the course of restoring democracy in Spain. Some leaders became obsessed with public opinion, and many columnists became governmental lackeys.

Like everything else in those days, freedom of the press recovered gradually. At the time of the first democratic election, in 1977, the government controlled all television transmissions, monopolized radio (private stations were forced to air Radio Nacional's official news bulletin), and maintained a vast network of local newspapers through the state-owned *Prensa del Movimiento*, as well through other significant public institutions.

The legislative activity of the Democratic Center Union (UCD), charged with restoring freedom of expression, was virtually nonexistent, probably because they assumed that the promulgation of the Constitution would offer sufficient guarantees. This caused confusion and allowed a few legal loopholes to crop up during the first two years of the transition. Fraga's law was not formally abolished, although the permit for newspaper publishing became a simple administrative procedure and the requirement of a press license was never enforced, despite the efforts of colleagues more concerned with the dignities of journalism than with its social vigor.

I remember the day we decided not to send ten copies of *El País* to the Ministry of Information two hours before distribution, as required. We thought it was an awkward and absurd mandate that merely gave the ministry's director general an opportunity to pressure, negotiate, or complain. We soon received a call from the ministry. I informed them that we were tired of government workers alerting the government or the competition about news that was about to be published in our newspaper. They understood and asked me to keep sending a few copies for the archives. A few days later the mandatory deposit of newspaper copies for preliminary inspection was formally abolished.

But government aggression continued in certain areas despite the reforms. Public Order Courts, judicial organisms specializing in political repression, continued their frenzied activity against the press. There were also court-martials, as well as smear campaigns against newspapers and publishing companies. This practice was as miserable as it was during the dictatorship, when it was more common. One well-known instance was the massive setup of don Fidel, Bishop of Calahorra, in revenge for his condemnation of totalitarianism. The police touched up several photographs to show him in bed with two prostitutes. The article ruined his reputation and his career as a bishop.

Fraga, during his self-proclaimed liberalizing era, led a campaign to slander José Antonio Novais, *Le Monde*'s correspondent in Spain, after unsuccessfully pressuring the newspaper to have him fired. His chronicles in the European press had allowed Spaniards to know what was happening in their country. Very few people did anything in Novais's defense.

The police and military intelligence services used defamation and slander as instruments of political influence well into the era of democracy, and they likely still do. I was once accused of belonging to the KGB. The military created false evidence, forged my signature in letters and on checks, and harassed me in a manner that was as vile as it was stupid. It must be remembered that, to a large extent, the dictator's bureaucracy was still in charge; the converts to democracy had to keep an eye on the guardians of orthodoxy. Many bureaucrats were eager to cover up traces of the past, and these anecdotes are illustrative of the atmosphere of these times.

It was finally the socialists, and not the alleged right-wing liberals, who accomplished the liberalization and privatization of the media. The government of Felipe González sold state newspapers to private enterprises, reorganized radio, and oversaw the creation of regional and private television stations. However, the socialists failed to initiate the same process with the EFE agency, which remained a stronghold of interventionism by the government, and left in place the statute of TVE (Spanish public television), which was approved during Suarez's presidency. The right wing, upon returning to power in 1996, shamelessly decided to keep Radio Televisión Española as an instrument of the government's vanity, a hub of corruption, and a costly squandering of public funds. Only with the return to power of the socialists, led by Rodríguez Zapatero, has reconstruction of Spanish public television advanced.

The naïveté of the government under Felipe González was surprising. Far from profiting or gaining strength through media privatization despite its long spell in power, the socialist government left the media to political opponents or representatives of opposing ideologies. González secured political power by riding a massive wave of popular support against Calvo-Sotelo's unstable tenure after the disaster of the February 23 coup (the attempted coup d'état, known as 23-F, began on February 23, 1981, and ended the following day). Those who witnessed Barack Obama's electoral victory in the United States can imagine the massive and enthusiastic support of the socialist victory in Spain in 1982.

The press actively participated in this victory (as in the case of Obama), yet the honeymoon did not last long. The first signs of the government's hardening stance with respect to the press emerged when accusations of corruption were made against the brother of Vice President Alfonso Guerra. It was at this time that Felipe González made his famous statement distinguishing public opinion from published opinion, discrediting the latter in favor of the former, a position supposedly endorsed by the votes received by the PSOE (Socialist Party). Although right, in a sense, he underestimated the fact that published opinion often becomes public opinion.

Prior to this episode, several other government skirmishes with newspapers had already taken place. I was involved in one of the most famous cases: a conflict with the minister of the interior, José Barrionuevo, caused by my newspaper's criticism of his antiterrorist policy and the crimes committed by the GAL (Antiterrorist Liberation Group), which at the time were applauded by most of the press, especially those who, fifteen years later, convinced Aznar to use this case to bring down González's government. However, despite their seriousness, such incidents weren't the result of premeditated harassment policies like those orchestrated later on. The transition from censorship to free press—in its widest sense, including all media—ended in the summer of 1989 when three private television licenses were granted.

That was the end of oppression, although some were determined to get a round-trip ticket. There is no explanation for José María Aznar's efforts to create and surround himself with loyal media that would praise his government's achievements and apply the paltry official doctrine to problems, large and small, that our country was facing. Today, democracy in Spain is solid, and liberties are guaranteed by institutions, but the People's Party government's aggression against dissidence and independent voices should not be forgotten.

In an era of free press, it is now surprising how easily a handful of journalists are able to blackmail a politician. Such journalists acknowledge no other truth, or ethics, but their own. These journalists have introduced an "anything goes" attitude to the press and successfully imposed ideological vacuity and irrational selfishness, while showing a complete lack of commitment to their readers and even themselves as journalists.

The Sogecable case is illustrative of José María Aznar's

attitude toward the media. The troubles began with the slim electoral victory of the People's Party in March 1996. Barely 300,000 votes separated the winner from runner-up Felipe González, and it was clear that Aznar would face a hard battle in establishing a government. His conversations with nationalist parties dragged on for months. In the meantime, many doubted that the little man with a moustache like Chaplin and the soul of an inquisitor would ever reach a parliamentary majority and be sworn in as president.

Amid this turmoil, *El País* published an editorial suggesting that although the PP had won the election, its leader was unable to set up a government cabinet, so perhaps other party leaders, such as Ruiz Gallardón, would be more effective in reaching an agreement and securing parliamentary support. Aznar has always considered Gallardón, Madrid's current mayor, to be a major rival and someone not worth trusting, and he was infuriated by this proposal. Aznar finally managed to secure support from Basque and Catalonian nationalists in an obscene display of political expediency by all parties involved, and from that moment on he believed that PRISA (one of Spain's largest media conglomerates and owner of *El País*) had no other objective than to remove him from power.

He was also convinced that the influence exerted by SER, Spain's largest radio network, (also owned by PRISA) was the main reason he had fallen short of an absolute majority. Significantly, it was a journalist acting as a presidential adviser who convinced Aznar that the substantial profits that PRISA realized from its pay-per-view television system would be used to weaken his government and finance González's return to the Moncloa. Goebbels said that big lies are easier to believe, and this speciousness was bought wholesale by the president, who initiated a war of extermination against the PRISA media group. He very nearly succeeded, thanks to the criminal complicity of a judge and the active cooperation of the cheerleaders of power.

Aznar's pressure on the media was not limited to the episode described above. He nearly banished the socialists from national television. He meddled in Telefónica's strategy of buying and creating channels, and in their subsequent sale to new owners, vetoing some candidates while favoring others. He used the power of the telecommunications monopoly, and that of other public companies privatized by him and run by his friends, to destroy the free market and reconfigure it as he saw fit.

His accomplice was the Communist Party, at the time obsessed with joining the right in a two-pronged attack against democratic socialism. Like a bull in a china shop, Aznar entered the pay-per-view business, destroyed soccer's financing model, and favored financial opportunists, all the while revealing a striking lack of respect, vision, or honor and a shameless lack of conviction. The grandson of one of the republic's most respected and most admired journalists in the twentieth century—despite his collaboration with the dictator—Aznar excelled at denying freedom of expression.

Shortly after Aznar became president, Jesús Polanco and I were asked to fire Eduardo Haro Tecglen from *El País* and also Iñaki Gabilondo from SER. We didn't, and thereafter Aznar refused to give any interviews to the media; this went on for years. Readers and listeners had never been more grateful.

After being exiled from the majority of platforms during his tenure as the leader of the opposition, then finally winning the 2004 elections, Rodríguez Zapatero was eager to promote the creation of new television networks in order to increase pluralism, thereby enhancing the left wing's presence. He was not entirely prudent in the methods he employed or the allies he chose. However, his efforts to build a respectable public television network are commendable. Communication policy has not been his strong suit, but it must be acknowledged that in his second term the president has been more aware of his mistakes and willing to learn from them.

True freedom in the media is rare, and it is always being threatened with extinction. Not everything in the golden era of Spanish journalism was wonderful. Political pressure certainly existed, as it always will with a healthy, independent media. However, I would argue that Spanish journalism's best moments occurred in the late 1970s and early 1980s, in terms of innovation, social respect, pluralism, and general professional excellence. To a large degree we exist now in the memory of this era, especially as conditions continue to deteriorate.

Despite the support of the media against political oppression, citizens increasingly find themselves defenseless against public attacks. The considerable number of defamatory actions speaks to the paltry state of our profession today. In Spain, where no specific libel laws exist, victims, lawyers, and judges hesitate to make a civil or criminal claim against abuse. The Constitutional Court's case law, despite creating an extensive and detailed *corpus doctrinae* on the subject, still has trouble addressing individual rights and the freedom of speech.

I have addressed this conflict on a number of occasions, particularly in my book *Cartas a un joven periodista* (*Letters to a Young Journalist*). The individual's vulnerability regarding the media sometimes results in blackmail at the hands of unscrupulous journalists. It is necessary to establish a legal framework with a minimum degree of objectivity, allowing journalists to know where they stand in their professional practice. Otherwise, freedom of information may turn into an authority used and abused by opportunists and know-it-alls.

As time goes on, consolidation of the press has encouraged criminal acts on the part of journalists, some of which, I'll admit, may have value for society at large. Resorting to such illegal methods is relatively frequent, and we must remind ourselves that journalists are neither spies nor policemen. Although I have stated that our profession has low-life origins, it also aspires to a higher truth, where honesty and transparency play an essential role.

And yet reality catches us by surprise. The proliferation and popularity of digital networks, their susceptibility to hackers, the vulnerability of communication, and the enormous diversity of technological innovation have generated new dangers and opportunities. Today, there is a plethora of online bulletins blending truth with lies, filled with defamation and acclamation, yet their arbitrariness goes unchecked.

The Parisian *canards* and the Italian *gazzettanti* would be ashamed of the abusive behavior and lack of quality on the Internet. Of course many sites are respectful, are professionally produced, and provide a real social function. However, most of them are nothing more than dumpsters filled with garbage. Nevertheless, analysts, financiers, big entrepreneurs, and even top politicians rely on these sites. No one seems able to stop the flow of junk mail into e-mail accounts. This situation must change. In a world where everything, from coffee to money to the transmission of knowledge, is instantaneous, justice cannot indulge the luxurious pace of judicial inquiry. Judicial procedures must be sped up, and the efficiency of the courts enhanced. Otherwise journalism could soon witness one of its darkest moments, living out Oscar Wilde's famous and caustic saying: "In the old days men had the rack. Now they have the press." And junk mail.

VALUE AND PRICE

IN 1983 A wave of excitement overtook editorial offices around the world. Prestigious newspapers were competing for Hitler's memoirs, an unparalleled publishing novelty, or, more precisely, one with only a few precedents that the short-term memory of journalists and media entrepreneurs failed to recall.

Despite their haste and thirst for victory, the *Sunday Times*, in 1968, exposed the forgery of Mussolini's diaries; the error cost the company a significant amount of money. A few years later, the same company was involved in an unsuccessful negotiation with Howard Hughes's representatives to acquire the millionaire's autobiography, after a fake one, written by the famous best-selling author Clifford Irving, had been published. The *Sunday Times* reporters who went to see Howard Hughes rejected the idea of publishing his autobiography because Hughes's people refused to allow comprehensive fact-checking.

Rupert Murdoch, owner and publisher of the *Times*, reacted in a peculiar manner when he discovered that the memoirs of the Nazi butcher were a hoax: his company trumpeted their publication. Some of his journalists were ashamed of having to publicly acknowledge their newspaper's mistake. "Well, in the end we are in the business of entertainment," Murdoch said.

Cynicism aside, Murdoch's statement might best define the times. I have written hundreds of pages and given dozens of talks on the digital revolution, only to realize that, as in the case of Murdoch, just a few words suffice to grasp the situation. The revolution involves a cocktail of information and entertainment, resulting from the preeminence of images and Wall Street's interest in the media. It is the marriage of *homo sapiens* and *homo videns* that has produced the new species, *homo ludens*.

Media enterprises have been forced to extend their

reach beyond the vital role of delivering information and have now become conglomerates for peddling leisure and entertainment. They are subject to the general rules of the market, but that should not be used as a pretext to forgo their private and public commitments to their readers and users.

A revolution like the one we are now facing will require the destruction of old values and the emergence of new ones. It is not a linear process, nor a defined one, but rather the product of an emerging reality. Experience is the only useful instrument for recognizing these new values, or for filling out the death certificate of old ones. Although some general principles do exist and should not be eliminated, other outdated values will lay claim to permanency simply to survive. This passion for permanence generates great uncertainty.

In classic value theory, as described by José Ferrater Mora in his *Diccionario de Filosofía*, the characteristics of value are the following: objectivity, mutual dependence, polarity, quality, and hierarchy. Even though the list has been debated many times, it can help us grasp the value of information providers in the new millennium. From an Aristotelian perspective, where any action or choice is aimed at attaining a good, and where the objective of the economy is wealth, it is not difficult to establish the existence of a business ethic with value emerging from production, irrespective of results. The poor reputation of business in our country—aside from criminal behavior—is due to a Catholic agrarian protectionism rather than a liberal free-market system. The term *value* has a specific and well-understood meaning under capitalism, as opposed to the term *bienes* (goods), used by the Physiocrats, from which the term *bienes raíces* (literally "root goods," real estate property) emerged with tragic undertones, as if it had something to do with Sartre's existentialism or the agony of Christianity.

The *ethos* of business is the creation of wealth. Profit making is legitimate but walks with a dubious halo within the moral universe where systems of wealth creation and distribution develop. This *ethos* is inherent to any productive activity, which includes the sharing of information, including information that might be considered detrimental to wealth creation. The objective of any company is to make money; the fact that many companies serve other communal interests essential to the establishment and function of democracy does not alter the fundamental truth of this assertion.

Therefore, criticism of those trafficking in information is frequently heard. One often hears protests that information has now become merchandise. In an advanced capitalist economy everything is merchandise, from food, shelter, and clothes to education and health care. Money, in addition to being an instrument of exchange, is also merchandise, as are art, poetry, and religion. Why should the press and media feel ashamed of making a profit? The press's only obligation is to observe the general rules of economics, as well as those that are particular and specific to its nature.

On the other hand, media companies work with raw material they do not own. They manage a public good and a common right that belongs to the citizens, and thus they are subject to limits and measures. At the same time, they must add value to their activities. Here we encounter the traditional problems of value theory, since it is difficult to establish whether such values are purely objective or depend on subjective interpretation. In the end, the question is whether we want things because they are valuable, or if things are valuable because we want them.

On one hand, large print runs, radio or television audiences, best-selling books, and blockbuster movies are all important goals for media companies. On the other hand, irrespective of how misunderstood or unsuccessful a writer might feel, he will never reject a readership. Distribution is a merit in itself in media companies, not only because of the profits they earn, but because of the boost it provides to the egos of their writers, whether they are book authors or journalists. Unfortunately, however, the media's credibility is hurt by their current "anything goes" attitude, in which they will take a chance on publishing anything that promises to sell. The invectives of media professionals and academics have little effect on public opinion, yet they have cast considerable doubt on the credibility of newspapers, radio, and television.

Overall, I think this discussion is unproductive. The duty of media companies is to their shareholders, which necessarily translates into maximizing sales. Yes, this does not mean that profit should be achieved by any method, or through the "anything goes" philosophy. There is no scarcity of professionals who value their decisions and the content they publish or programs they produce according to demand. Unfortunately, this argument is less acceptable regarding bad television, and intolerable with respect to public television and radio. The counterargument is that they are to be seen and heard as public goods rather than a means of exerting a fundamental right.

This distinction is essential and has fueled intense debates in the past century, particularly on occasion of Nobel laureate Seán MacBride's 1980 report on behalf of UNESCO titled "Many Voices, One World." It seems to me that the correct approach to this issue is to consider information as the right of individuals—both the right to inform other people and the right to be informed by institutions and public administrations. It is not, however, the only possible approach, and the educational value of the media is undeniable, particularly in emerging societies subject to an exclusively Western point of view.

The role of the state in guaranteeing access to information should be limited to regulation. Anything else is, generally, a manifestation of the government's desire to manipulate the media. Calling television a public service—as it is referred to in Spain—is a means by which the media justifies the government's arbitrariness. According to this classification, broadcasting is supposedly based on quality, which often isn't the case.

Independence is another value commonly attributed to successful media companies. A newspaper's credibility depends on the validity of its content. Such dependence is increasingly difficult to maintain in the twenty-first century. According to my dictionary, the etymology of independence is *summa libertas*, which implies a lack of bonds and commitments, which of course is impossible today, and which in turn indicates the decadence, and corruption, of the media.

Independence often has a cheerful connotation. During the last twenty-five years of the twentieth century, *El País* hit the streets with a slogan under its masthead that read, "Independent morning daily." Our intention as the founders was to publicly express freedom from commitment, ideological or otherwise. *El País* was created on a shoestring budget amid enormous technical problems, using a rotary press incapable of meeting demand. The newspaper was always late, sometimes not appearing on the newsstands before noon. When people asked who or what the newspaper was independent of, we would answer sarcastically, "As it says on the cover, it is independent of the morning."

Not long ago, on the occasion of a substantial change at the newspaper (maybe the first since it was founded), we thought the time had come to eliminate the "independent" slogan. Not because we were no longer independent, but because we believed that it was no longer a particularly distinctive representation amid the plethora of media flooding the market. Javier Moreno, the newspaper's executive editor, suggested substituting "global Spanish daily," which was enthusiastically embraced. There was no better definition for the project that has inspired all of us for decades.

People cast aspersions on the label "independent media" because everyone answers to someone. You're gonna have to serve somebody, as Bob Dylan wrote. It's hard to argue with this in the so-called real world.

In the real world there are countless positions and ambiguities that lie among arrogant journalists (particularly those in radio and television) who claim nobody has a right to tell them what to do or say and the ridiculous conjecture that the media is simply the voice of those holding the purse strings. Media independence exists only to the extent that owners and publishers maintain the personalities of their outlets. As Roy Thomson said when he owned the London *Times*:

I emphatically declare that no person or group can buy or use influence to gain editorial support from any newspaper in the Thomson group. Each newspaper is able to perceive the public's interest on its own, and will do so without any advice, recommendation or indication from Thomson's central organization. I do not believe that a publication can be adequately managed if its editorial pages are not independently and freely directed by a professional journalist of great capacity and complete dedication. This has been and will continue to be my policy.

Such independence is an asset.

A company's profitability helps maintain independence. As long as they don't subsist on public or private subsidies to survive, newspaper personnel will be protected from editorial decisions taken autonomously by publishers and editorial staff. This is something that has traditionally been poorly understood by journalists, many of whom maintain a romantic, almost bohemian, view of their profession and believe that poverty is an inescapable prerequisite for freedom. These same romantics might believe that freedom is expensive, since they believe that everyone can be bought. A newspaper that sacrifices profitability for the obsessions or stubbornness of its publisher is as doomed to fail as the newspaper that pursues profit at the expense of integrity. A virtuous circle can be maintained when editorial independence becomes a business value and profitability guarantees independence.

A newspaper publisher is like the administrator of public property: he has the right to receive information. The real question is how he performs this endeavor. Important decisions are made constantly at a daily newspaper. Frequently decisions must be made without consultation. Often decisions are made by well-trained journalists or producers familiar with the content, yet not always aware of the economic consequences of their actions and the effects those actions might have on the company. In the short term, management happens in a matter of hours, and sometimes minutes. Managers should manage and journalists should write.

Once successfully established, media has proven to be one of the most durable industries. Implementation of long-term planning, investment, and forecasting is fairly easy as well. There are few products and brands in the world with a history of more than 100 or 200 years. Such exclusivity enables short-term decisions and long-term strategies, as well as oversight that prevents management from harming the company's future.

Those outside of the business are often surprised with our quick decision-making. Among virtues (values?) innate to the journalistic enterprise are flexible hours and flexible relationships between publishers and employees; authority based on knowledge and expertise rather than title; an understanding of the "customer"; and the social aspect of content and entertainment.

Continuity in staff is a two-pronged approach: generating immediate results and charting the general course of the company. Staff stability is an essential condition for the sustained growth of an entrepreneurial project. Such continuity might result in decadence, yet it often leads to texture and character.

The basis of any entrepreneurial success is remaining faithful to a project, which requires determination and patience, qualities not often found in the business schools. Human capital—the talent—is critical to creating profit. Generally speaking, the development of large and complex business conglomerates emerged first with simple ideas, such as finding a loyal readership, carving out a topical niche, and achieving sufficient scale. There are two basic requirements for a leading newspaper: credibility and independence. Profitability guarantees the latter and is the basis of quality. A newspaper endeavor can be summed up as an agreement among its readers, its journalists, and its shareholders; anything less results in failure.

Traditionally, newspapers must cultivate readers and advertisers. Often their interests converge; just as often, conflict emerges. Government advertising and advertising by state-owned companies are often used to influence editorial opinions, although private advertisers are not above such coercion. Journalists generally know that advertising is essential. It is not the enemy but rather an ally. Almost half a century ago, Marshall McLuhan explained that, sociologically, advertising is good since it provides information on a sale at your local department store, or the premiere of the latest Batman movie. A newspaper without advertising is boring.

These two markets have been joined by a third that shows surprising strength: promotional inserts. European newspapers have been losing readers at a rate close to 1 million per year on average, and this crisis in circulation has strengthened the trend toward inserts. Initially, promotional inserts were meant to increase customer loyalty and boost sales. They were designed to capture a readership that otherwise would not buy their newspaper, particularly young people.

Such methods have produced revenue but not necessarily profits, because it is indispensable to inform the public, via television, that tomorrow, along with news and entertainment, a Barbie doll or instant soup is forthcoming. In 2006, the Spanish newspaper industry devoted 12 percent of its revenue to finance promotional campaigns totaling 334 million euros.

Many ask how long this craze is going to last, perhaps because their memories don't go back 100 years. Newspapers are a good way to sell goods and services. The agility and speed, the direct relationship with the customer, and the fluidity of information about the popularity of each product are unbeatable.

Of course, profitability is not everything, as we have demonstrated. A newspaper must be free from ideological bonds, personal commitments, prejudices, passions, and phobias. This does not mean that newspapers shouldn't have opinions. An independent newspaper is neither aseptic nor eclectic, and its points of view are relatively predictable. Independence also entails transparency, something often forgotten by managers. Public identification with the owners of a newspaper is important. Opacity works against credibility. The public has a right to know a newspaper's financial standing, its objectives, its circulation figures, its journalists, and the general evolution of the business. This is even more important regarding state-owned enterprises, which paradoxically tend to be most secretive.

However independent newspapers may be, they should not shun their readership or the general community that they serve. Indeed, newspapers must embody the general principles of the community they serve. Any self-respecting media company must defend principles, such as one person's freedom ends where another's begins. For this reason, they must weigh freedoms and choose between competing freedoms, which isn't easy.

Apart from reporting the lives we live, the communities and worlds we create by being together, the media contributes to those worlds, creates its own values, sometimes to a disturbing degree. In any case, the truths of the media do not always coincide with the philosopher's truth.

For example, television exerts an enormous influence on fashion and spending habits, and radio manipulates our use of language. Bad taste, vulgarity, triviality, and the less literary side of grotesqueness are largely due to a few television programs, but also to yellow journalism and the people who shape culture generally. The appeal of certain American television series is so great that the Spanish public is more familiar with the procedural aspects of the judicial or forensic systems in the United States than those in their own country. The growing homogenization of lifestyles and behaviors brought about by globalization represents a serious threat to the cultural identities of sovereign powers. Even when dubbed into Spanish, Catalonian, or Basque, Hollywood's message and values are constant. Paradoxically, Hollywood's influence will only increase as it moves into local and regional markets, due to the use of native languages.

Journalism's interests and values are frequently in conflict with those of Wall Street and other financial structures. Such conflicts are also common between journalism and education and health care. News that is known to be false should not be published; conversely, news that is in the public interest should not be censored, even if it adversely affects the government, a lobby, a newspaper owner, or the professional staff that works for him. After all, we are not dealing with extravagant or utopian behavior.

Again, the greatest contradictions and challenges emerge from the digital revolution. Due to the large number of new technical applications and news channels, information is available to everybody, often for free. It seems not to matter that analysis, interpretation, and data coordination would add value to that information. Also, conglomeration continues. Media companies now control newspapers; radio and television broadcasting networks; film production, distribution, and exhibition companies; software companies; and telecommunication companies. Size seems to add value through economy of scale and increased access to content, yet it tends to compromise independence, transparency, and the diffusion of power, all important to democracy.

There is no empirical proof for this last statement. On the contrary, the existence of many large companies enables the survival of small newspapers, and this may represent a guarantee of independence for local and regional organizations. On the other hand, it would be ridiculous to deny the risks or threats that arise from too much concentration. We also have to understand that in a globalized world we need to compete globally, which only companies of a certain size can do efficiently.

Media companies now combine news with entertainment,

as Murdoch boasted. There is no reason to be concerned. Chesterton rightfully said that "fun" is not the opposite of "serious"; "fun" is the opposite of "boring," and in the *Siglo de Oro* (Golden Century), Tirso de Molina, the dramatist and poet, was devoted to "instructing while entertaining."

Journalists must be able to mix thought with fun, denunciation with dilettantism, and pleasure with responsibility. Entertainment now covers all aspects of our lives; *homo ludens* has achieved primacy. There is no shortage of people who believe that one of the objectives of a democracy is entertainment, as the Lewinsky affair demonstrated. We have gone from "There is no business like show business" to "There is no business without show business."

Some of these assertions may disappoint or scandalize those who, quite rightly, regard freedom of expression as a basic element of democracy. I will only add that democracy will be strengthened by these new developments as long as we approach them with curiosity and a critical spirit, but without hostility. Old prejudices and passions will give way to new points of view and passions.

The media's main asset is human capital. The future of organizations that work with thoughts and ideas, with *content*—such a slippery and delicate, yet powerful, word—depends on the existence of well-trained, serious-minded individuals. As long as there are journalists, producers, writers, and script writers capable of interpreting the desires and moods of the people, and as long as there are imaginative people with passion and understanding, media companies and the media world in general will continue to play an important and essential role in society, in the enjoyment of freedom.

ASSASSINS

BETWEEN 1090 AND 1272 several groups of Ishmaelites combined forces to fend off the Crusader invasion of the territories known today as Syria. Like today's fundamentalists, these people were ferocious and willing to sacrifice their lives to defend their holy land against the infidels. Before combat they smoked hashish. This is the origin of the *hashishin*, or hashish users, whose name was transformed into *asesino*, *assasin*, *assasino* in the Romance languages. An assassin is a murderer of his fellow men, someone who uses violence against others as an end in itself, and who operates under the effects of outside stimulants or inducements.

I owe the etymology of this term to Georgetown University professor Bruce Hoffman, a widely acclaimed expert on terrorism who has spent years studying its relationship to religious movements. His book *Inside Terrorism* was published in 1998 by Columbia University Press. In it, Hoffman illustrates the fact that terrorism has always had roots in ideological, political, or religious fanaticism, and that terrorists are not necessarily idealistic, as some stubbornly insist, but obsessive individuals manipulated to the point of psychopathology.

Classic terrorism can be distinguished from other forms of institutional or personal violence in many ways. First, the terrorist pursues notoriety and publicity, and seeks to create terror among populations; second, the terrorist objectifies his or her victims; and finally, terrorism is organized and finds support among groups that, despite condemning the methods employed by terrorism, often understand its reasons and even share its objectives.

Something similar occurred in Israel during the first century, when the zealots organized into bands of *sicarii*, a word used today to describe terrorists under the command of Colombian drug lords. The Israelite *sicarii* acted in broad daylight, publicly killing any representative of

Roman power in occupied Palestine and their own countrymen who were collaborating with the Romans. Making one's name known and getting people's attention are at the core of contemporary terrorist activities: the only difference today is the role played by the mass media, which confers terrorist acts with a resonance that would have been unimaginable until recently.

There is widespread agreement that the terrorist's objective is public opinion, which is what distinguishes it from other forms of violence, like torture, for example. Umberto Eco has asserted that "terrorism is a phenomenon of the era of mass media. If there was no mass media there would be no events intended to become news." Marshall McLuhan stated that "without communication there would be no terrorism." Brian Michael Jenkins, who wrote a book on international terrorism and world security, points out that "terrorists want a lot of people watching, not a lot of people dead." Terrorism is essentially an act of communication; its importance is not in the direct damage inflicted—however severe—but in the message. Terrorists are not interested in their victims as much as in the video of their victims, if you will. Victims represent a bloody and necessary instrument for conveying their message.

Politicians and journalists often state that the objectives of terrorists are death and destruction, and hence their acts are devoid of rationality. I understand the purpose of such an argument, but not the logic. The fact that a murderer's reasoning is different from that of the rest of us does not indicate a lack of reason. Terrorists know what they are doing when they kill innocent people in an indiscriminate and brutal manner. They know the scope of the message they are sending to the rest of society. Worse, they are aware of the effectiveness of their approach. Any other interpretation is naïve and won't help address the problem of terrorism.

Modern terrorism's petri dish is the media. The digital society is its ally and, paradoxically, its primary victim: the purpose of terrorism is to affect public opinion through terror, suspicion, and fear. This is the reason why military experts, policemen, politicians, judges, and social researchers are concerned about the media's role with respect to terrorism.

We are dealing here with a delicate issue involving consciousness, deeply rooted convictions, and all kinds of emotions, especially in countries like Spain, where the blood of the victims of ETA and Muslim fundamentalists awakens calls for justice and reparation. As a journalist, I have very often encountered the effects of terrorism. I have attended conferences, international seminars, and symposia on the subject, and I believe I can make a useful contribution that runs contrary to customary stereotypes emerging from political manipulation and intellectual stubbornness. I am interested in denouncing clichés used to justify certain attitudes or support questionable decisions in the fight against terrorism.

Perhaps the most common assertion is that all terrorism is the same since there is no good terrorism. Such statements can be found in the speeches of politicians and those fighting organized crime. It was also an opinion shared liberally by President Aznar while he was the head of government in Spain. While I agree that there is no good terrorism, I also believe that, despicable as it is, terrorism has different faces, despite ideological or operational connections. Here are five different typologies:

1. **Terrorism based on ideological or religious fanaticism.** This is clearly the case with al Qaeda, responsible for the attack on the World Trade Center and the Pentagon, and the bombing of

the Atocha train station in Madrid. But it is also the case with Hamas, as well as the Jewish fanatics from Gush Emunim (Bloc of the Faithful), who see giving up Israeli territory as an act of sacrilege. One of its members murdered Yitzhak Rabin in 1995 during an election rally. That Muslim fundamentalism thrives in impoverished areas or in countries exploited by foreign intervention or local politicians is closely related to the lack of hope in the lives of inhabitants. As with their Iranian counterparts of the past, the Iraqi and Palestinian teenagers who inflict pain on the enemy and sacrifice themselves as human bombs have nothing to lose. They do not regard their own life as something worth preserving; instead, they aspire to Paradise, where they will be rewarded. They are beyond physical coercion, and thus the fight against terrorism requires more than simple police measures; it calls for social and educational policies that improve the outlook and lives of these would-be martyrs dispossessed since birth.

Religious fundamentalism is not limited to terrorist movements. In the mid-twentieth century, the Franco regime labeled its war effort a "crusade," and in the first years of this millennium we witnessed an American president repeatedly invoke the name of God to justify the armed invasion of Iraq, under the pretext of liberating its people from the yoke of Saddam Hussein.

2. **Ideological terrorism,** like that of the famous Italian Red Brigades, Direct Action in France, or the Baader-Meinhof band in Germany. Some of their traits are also shared by the old Argentine Montoneros—the Peronist urban guerrilla group. Instead of religious fanaticism, these groups seek to address a historical grievance. Their members, or at least their leaders, are often intellectuals, and their ranks often include young people from wealthy families. They normally choose their victims from among the leaders or representatives of the opposition: it is a clear and emphatic way to convey their agenda, which seems suffused with anarchist nostalgia.

3. **Terrorism linked to nationalistic or territorial claims,** which also includes Palestinian terrorism—aside from its fundamentalist identity. Other representatives include ETA, the IRA, and the Chechen movements. This type of violent activism receives an important level of support from the general population. Despite the violence, many consider the claims of such groups legitimate because of their objectives and the allegedly oppressive state violence directed against them.

4. **Counterterrorism or state terrorism,** which is financed by public funds and carried out on behalf of the government, when not a part of its institutional policy, as is the case in Israel. It is sometimes carried out by security forces or armies, but in the majority of cases it requires the services of mercenaries, paid for through secret funds managed by governments or other public institutions. This category includes the Argentine Triple A, Brazil's paramilitary squads, Batallón Vasco Español, and GAL in

Spain. Even James Bond fits in this category.

The justification by governments for using the mafia to fight terrorism is not so different from arguments defending the invasion of Iraq by Anglo-American forces. Ironically, this position tends to reinforce the dialectical position of terrorists who insist they are waging a war against a state. If this were so, and accepting that this conflict would be far more insidious, complicated, and threatening than a traditional war, the state would be entitled to use the same methods as its subversive enemies.

From this point of view, the excess in judicial guarantees for all types of criminals in democratic states would represent a weak spot, and would hamper the effectiveness of those defending legality. This is the reason for the existence of the legal limbo with respect to Guantánamo, where hundreds of prisoners are incarcerated on the basis of their suspected connections to al Qaeda. The legalization of torture in the United States, as per President Bush's instructions, pursued the same motives and represented one of the most ominous government crimes ever committed by its leader. President Obama's decision to close Guantánamo and his prohibition against cruel methods in the name of freedom are restoring hope for those of us who believe that the United States is one of the great protectors of human rights and democratic principles.

5. **Individual terrorism,** the description of which contradicts one of the main traits usually associated with this phenomenon (i.e., that it is carried out by an organized group). It is rare, but has sometimes proven deadly, as in the case of the Unabomber; or socially damaging, as in the distribution of anthrax through the mail in the United States.

There are surely other typologies (for instance, the Colombian FARC don't fit any one of the categories above), and we could establish many subdivisions within each type. My intention is only to show that there are myriad types of terrorism. They cannot be treated in the same manner, neither by politicians nor by the media. Fighting the ETA is not the same as fighting al Qaeda, and combating al Qaeda is not the same as combating FARC or GAL.

The variable nature of terrorist groups and their motivations also explains the irrefutable fact that those considered terrorists by some are regarded as national heroes, spiritual leaders, or courageous guerrillas by others. In Spain, there was confusion when Aznar used the term *Basque National Liberation Movement* in public to refer to ETA and its entourage, when such an expression has never been used by the media, aside from the Basque newspaper *Gara* and its predecessor, *Egin*. The solemn declaration that all terrorism is equal could only emanate from the *pensée unique* in its avid search for immediate and definitive solutions to a complex problem that rejects simplification, both politically and with respect to countermeasures. The only realm where all terrorists are equal is the moral realm, which is miserable.

Another cliché asserts that since the media enables the propaganda effect of terrorists by publicizing their actions, silence or a sort of self-censorship would facilitate the prosecution of terrorism and prevent its proliferation. There is no evidence supporting this argument. Indeed, there is abundant proof refuting it. It is increasingly difficult to silence events—even in countries like China. If countries censor terrorism, terrorists might respond by increasing attacks in order to get noticed. The general consensus among journalists is that terrorism-related events should be dealt with in the same manner as other important news, using the same rigor, honesty, and respect for the readership. The golden rule is to verify the facts and to serve the interests of our readers, viewers, or listeners. This entails avoiding generalizations and establishing an effective case history, which is how all news should be covered.

This view is not shared by everybody. The Assembly of the Council of Europe, established in 1979, states that "the media, when reporting on terrorist incidents, should accept the self-restraint required to balance the public's right to be informed with the duty to avoid giving help to the terrorists by unduly publicizing their activities." During the 1980s Margaret Thatcher and Felipe González demanded that terrorists "be starved of the oxygen of publicity they demand," in the words of the British prime minister. Establishing the line betwcen propaganda and news is always a controversial endeavor, but journalists must treat terrorism just as they treat any other event, with informative rigor and social responsibility.

Another assumption is that publishing interviews with terrorists or broadcasting their communiqués is a form of cooperation. Heads of media companies are known to struggle with this decision, especially regarding television. As noted, I believe that generalizations aren't useful. Terrorists have often demanded that their statements be published, with threats of killing hostages or as a condition for their release.

Censorship is a violation of freedom of speech, and we must not surrender to this type of blackmail. Yet when two fundamental rights are in conflict, decision-makers must choose the lesser of two evils. I have always defended victims' safety and right to life. That is why I have supported paying ransoms. I believe that terrorism can only be fought using analysis, intelligence, and commitment, not by some rigid political stance.

Those who have suffered directly from terrorism should receive all the human comfort and economic support possible, and should be spared political manipulation. Unfortunately, reparations are often scarce and irregular; victims of different terrorist attacks are treated differently, and it is difficult to address legal claims on behalf of victims. Throughout the past few decades I have met dozens of people who were threatened, including businessmen, politicians, journalists, and judges, and who received no help from the police. Many resorted to private companies to protect themselves.

Political exploitation of terrorist victims is always unfortunate. An indisputable example of such exploitation was the tribute celebrated at Las Ventas (the famous bull ring) in Madrid to memorialize the kidnapping and murder of Miguel Ángel Blanco. The generosity of the people and their feelings of solidarity were manipulated for political purposes. We witnessed the extent to which show business, theatrics, and publicity invade even the most solemn occasions.

I was taught as a young reporter that it was immoral to exploit other people's suffering for the sake of increasing newspaper sales or winning votes. Since we were living under a dictatorship, these admonishments usually applied to the coverage of horrific and criminal events. Some photographers shamelessly exploited victims in the attempt to capture uniquely expressive, but ultimately sensational, images.

Today, family members of those killed by terrorists

commonly complain of privacy infringement because the event and their subsequent suffering are repeatedly shown on television. Occasionally, relatives of the victims even learn of the tragic event through the media. Far too often a father learns that his son has been killed in a terrorist attack from the people thrusting a camera and a microphone in his face. Thus, the sobriety and respect shown by the American media toward the victims of September 11 were admirable. Not a single body appeared on television. Supporting the victims involves protecting and honoring them; it means not exploiting them. We should remember that, from a political point of view, victims are not the objective of terrorists, but rather its instrument. The objective is society, generalized terror.

For the same reasons, the attitude that we must remain neutral and report on events without getting involved is unacceptable. It's one thing to try to unveil the motives of terrorists, to analyze their opinions, psychology, and the roots of their actions; it's another to remain distant or aloof. We are facing a sinister and deadly threat against freedom. Those of us who believe in democracy are determined to defend it, and we will not forget the damage caused by terrorism.

The above paragraph might be useful for those who have to deal with the media in the context of terrorism. As I've said, no two terrorist situations are identical; each one must be analyzed separately. I have personally faced many demands by terrorists and in many situations have been requested by governments to remain silent or even lie for reasons of state security. The sanctity of human life has been my guiding principle, above all other arguments, however reasonable or lofty they might have been. Personal freedom and the right to live trump all other considerations in times of doubt or deliberation.

The security of citizens in a democracy is a difficult issue that cannot be addressed by dictatorial methods. The fight against state terrorism in a democracy is subject to the law, and criminals often take advantage of these restrictions to escape justice. Governments are too often tempted to seek more efficient methods and morally questionable shortcuts when fighting terrorism.

Security in a democracy involves the absence of risks in the exercise of freedom. To a great extent, we feel secure even amid indecision and ambiguity if we are standing on firm ground. Security also arises from a defensive instinct, which presupposes the use of force. We often hear politicians and opinion leaders saying that the exercise of democracy consists of attaining an adequate balance between security and freedom. However, we must be wary of such statements, since they end up establishing justifications for limits on personal liberties. An absolutely secure and risk-free exercise of these liberties would paradoxically entail a renunciation of the freedom to enjoy them.

One should also question "national security" as a reason to curtail freedom. The only concept of security compatible with our current legal system would be one aimed at strengthening democratic rights and liberties. The fact that the state does not violate any constitutional rights in the course of maintaining order is not enough. The state must be organized to preserve such principles. Any other attitude is illegitimate and immoral.

Journalists are continually tested by government leaders who justify their demands for silence, manipulation, and censorship in the name of the higher good of collective security. The professional and moral duty of journalists is to tell the truth and to report events as they're witnessed, not to silence them. It's unacceptable to burden journalists with evaluating the consequences of publishing an article.

All this does not mean that journalists are or should be insensitive to the general good or that they should not assess the damage that might be caused by their publications. A journalist is a citizen, and it is logical and understandable that he or she should weigh the interests of his or her community when making a decision. However, establishing this as a rule is impossible. The choice of whether or not to heed a government's demand not to publish something must be considered on a case-by-case basis, according to the specific circumstances. In this realm, I have always favored respecting the autonomy of newspaper publishers.

The frequent meddling of politicians in the media under the pretext of the war on terror is useless, and it represents a serious threat to our civil liberties.

THE GLOBAL PARADOX

FREEDOM OF THE press emerged from nineteenth-century liberal democratic movements. The ruling elites of the civilized world belonged to a learned society, where newspapers, the privileged hosts of political debate, were local or national phenomena, almost invariably anchored by nationalist feelings. Newspapers played a vital role in sparking the bourgeois revolutions, a role as important as, if not more important than, the encyclopedia's service to the Enlightenment. But back then newspapers were still, quite simply, vessels for the exchange of ideas or experiences.

The media performs an essential role amid globalization.

It is simultaneously its cause and effect, while also contributing to the creation of a new social paradigm. The financial crisis that began with the subprime mortgage bust revealed not a circumstantial failure in the system, but rather a structural change and the birth of a new paradigm based on the massive and chaotic use of advanced technologies. Digitization has reduced what formerly was composed of several different elements to a single ingredient: bytes. This simple concept explains the convergent character of this emerging culture (the interaction of text, data, animated images, and sounds). Artificial satellites, digital television, new methods of knowledge management, and so many other contributions are shaping a world in which the Internet, the network of networks, has become the basic element.

Despite thousands of articles written about the Internet, numerous research projects and symposia devoted to it, and the efforts of public and private institutions to understand what it will mean for society, few comprehensive theories of the digital revolution have emerged. The world was brimming with optimism for the future of advanced technologies just before the dot-com crash. Now that optimism is guarded, to say the least. No one doubts that the Internet is the future. We have short memories and seem to have forgotten that the technological bubble introduced a catastrophe of considerable proportions.

In 1999, Internet-related industries generated 25 percent of new employment in the United States. In the first two months of 2000 the sector lost 35,000 jobs, and 75 percent of its value on the stock market. Despite this, Bill Gates claimed that the first ten years of the new century would be known as the digital decade. Of course, he was right. The record industry no longer exists as we once knew it; instead, music is downloaded from the Net. Telecommunications now offers services and features never imagined before; cell phones have become a major vehicle for the news. The state's great postal monopolies have disappeared or have been privatized and transformed beyond recognition. E-mail and texting have become universal. Some other forecasts will take longer to become manifest, like e-books or the disappearance of paper billing by businesses, although change will arrive before we expect it. Some of us continue to resist the all-encompassing aspects of living in the digital world.

A few years ago I tried to establish a few principles

that summarize this new situation, and I will attempt to do so again. These concepts were described in an essay I wrote in 1999 for the Club of Rome, a global think tank dealing with international political issues, and it is surprising how many of them are still valid:

1. **The digital society is global**: it does not have geographical or temporal boundaries, despite the benefits it provides to local communities.

2. **The digital society is convergent:** it is the place where all kinds of knowledge meet. It is the herald of a new epistemology.

3. **The digital society is interactive:** it is based on dialogue and cooperation among people, thus the incredible success of social networks.

4. **The digital society is chaotic:** it does not accept established hierarchies and is not subject to the usual standards of authority. This is a time for libertarians, but also for sophists and charlatans.

5. **The digital society is the cradle of a new virtual reality,** which is not just an imagined reality: it exists in an objective manner. During the most recent economic crisis, billions of dollars' worth of financial wealth evaporated as quickly and as thoroughly as it was created, virtually.

6. **The digital society is swift:** it develops quickly and in a nearly autonomous manner, exceeding all expectations of growth.

7. **The digital society is paradoxical,** and exists amid contradictions. Despite being convergent, the new culture favors fragmentation; being global, it enjoys many local versions; it is interactive, yet it favors isolation and solipsism; though chaotic, it leads to an abrasive homogenization.

The digital revolution is linked to the density of telephone networks and global telecommunications traffic. Most of this traffic is concentrated in the United States, Europe, Japan, and Australia, while China and India are catching up. Entire regions of the planet, especially Africa and much of Latin America, have yet to partake in the revolution. In many ways, the Internet is for the privileged. If this phenomenon is not addressed by authorities and governments, it may promote division among regions, countries, and citizens; the rich and the knowing versus the poor and the unknowing.

Something similar occurred during the industrial revolution. The enormous wealth generated over the last 200 years has been distributed very unevenly. In rich countries, the standard of living has improved twenty-fold since 1800; in the poorest and more populated countries the figure is 2.5. The Internet offers opportunity for accelerated economic development. I do not believe in the neutral character of technology, and it is difficult for me to accept that its qualities, positive and negative, are entirely dependent on man.

Yet I also have little sympathy for Luddites. As Professor Manuel Castells, a Spanish sociologist, has pointed out, technology, or lack thereof, reflects the capacity of a society to transform itself. Scientific and technological progress offers many solutions to the desperate search for happiness in which billions of human beings take part.

The digital revolution and the Internet allow us to imagine perspectives never before dreamed of through the exchange of knowledge, in conversations between cultures, in the convergence of civilizations. The revolution promotes what might be called a planetary consciousness, along with a sort of universal ethics, which lends itself to helping the disenfranchised.

Since the Internet is an intrinsically global and interactive phenomenon, new technologies are strongly influencing how the world communicates about issues related to the economy (especially finance), education, and the dissemination of information and news. The digital revolution has energized globalization, sometimes to the point of paroxysm, certainly beyond what we've already witnessed, with respect to food, fashion, cars, and leisure. It will also contribute to advances in virtual reality. Virtual boundaries will become vague, incoherent, paradoxical, and fluid. New links will be found for network communities, some of which will be unrecognizable, others that will reinforce traditional identities. Hence, the role of language as a vehicle for communication and a system for social and individual identification is reinforced.

The press, which played a critical role in democracy's

progress, as I've shown, will recede into the background, mainly because of the global nature of the Internet and the eminence of the image. Unfortunately, this demotion will be at the expense of written culture and literacy.

Today, the media is contributing to the socialization of habits and cultures on a planetary scale, but it often clashes with diverse traditions and rules. A global regulation of the right to inform is difficult to imagine in a world divided by beliefs, taboos, and conflicting interests. Substantial disparities in existing national legislations, as well as religious and cultural differences, represent nearly insurmountable obstacles for attaining agreement that may enjoy a wide consensus. But if some kind of regulation is not agreed on, the distortions and abuses of this right, or its partial suppression in the name of other principles, can end up stifling democracy. We have recently experienced this with respect to the current financial turmoil: a global society demands global rules, as well as authorities that are able to enforce compliance. It is also worth noting the difficulties that lie in the implementation of such a task in the field of copyright and intellectual property rights, for instance. A declaration of principles is insufficient: coercive measures for enforcement are necessary.

The impracticality of a coercive application of the law is the greatest impediment to regulating the Internet. China and Australia attempt to prohibit access to thousands of Web pages for political, sexual, or moral reasons, but these control measures are demagogic and inefficient. Lawmakers must be aware of the changes brought on as a result of such measures: the fact that code is being replaced by software, and whoever controls software writes the rules.

Ever since the telecommunications industry was deregulated, mergers, partnerships, acquisitions, and all sorts of financial operations have shaken up the market. Information companies, film producers, software providers, and telecommunications and cable companies have entered into joint ventures or have merged, often betraying one another in search of a global market and economy of scale. We are facing a formidable concentration process.

The digital society favors the creation of huge conglomerates that aspire to global domination. As Negroponte said, there are no frontiers for bytes, nor are there any customs agents to investigate them or imprison them. Along with huge technological capacities, these companies accumulate immense financial resources and generally operate in a variety of countries with very different cultures, legal systems, and developmental levels. While integration within media conglomerates grows and their worldwide presence increases, there is a trend toward single companies accumulating and managing both content and distribution.

Ownership concentration in the media is correlated with globalization, and everything seems to indicate that it will intensify in the coming years. This is disturbing, and we must be prepared to address the challenges it poses, instead of refusing to acknowledge the trend and its inevitable outcome. Paradoxically, there will also be a proliferation of small information companies and private enterprises that benefit from the very same technological advances that favor the creation of large conglomerates. The existence of very few and very powerful worldwide information networks should not put an end to the emergence of local or regional organizations that guarantee pluralism and democratic rights. However, citizens' access to media might be curtailed even further, so the right to inform could turn into the privilege of a professional caste, rather than something available to any citizen of the free world.

The increased capacity for transmitting informational,

artistic, or entertainment programs is not being met by supply; there is a lack of content. This has become the strategic cornerstone for the market's main agents, who ignore one of the most unique traits of the digital age: decisions must be based on demand. Copyright accumulation has allowed media companies to acquire vast quantities of content in order to build enormous catalogs to which they are guaranteed exclusive commercialization. They have recently become involved in copyright production as well: broadcasting rights for sporting events have increased in importance. Football (European and American), boxing, tennis, and many other sports, along with pornography, are the real engines for new consumption technologies. Research in the copyright field is proceeding apace, since legal shortcomings are now provoking serious concern among cultural producers and media conglomerates.

Fundamentally, globalization is a consequence of technological innovation rather than administrative and political deregulation. Deregulation was inevitable, though policies of plentiful liquidity and nearly negative interest rates have heavily favored the development of the media industry, which has tried to grow in all directions at once and taken on excessive levels of debt to do so. This was not a fad but rather a real offensive designed to conquer an uncertain future, where the role of newspapers in the world of communication is becoming more and more diffuse.

Times are hard for newspapers; jobs are being cut, companies are going out of business, mastheads are disappearing. The end of the paper edition of the *Christian Science Monitor*, which has been published for more than 100 years, the bankruptcy of the *Chicago Tribune* and the *Los Angeles Times*, and the difficult situation faced by the *New York Times* and *Le Monde* seem to indicate the end of an era in which newspapers served as the touchstones of public opinion in advanced democracies.

Are we facing the demise of the newspaper? It is difficult to imagine, particularly for those of us who have spent our lives in the business. A couple of years ago at a public event in Madrid, I confessed, much to the puzzlement of many in the audience, that if I were to found *El País* today I would do it online, and only maybe publish a paper version. This statement was not a joke. It is rooted in a firm conviction that the world of newspapers as we have known it is coming to an end. They will no longer be the sort of vertically integrated industrial empires where all power relations were socialized.

Of course, I hope that newspapers continue to exist, but their nature, the business model, their approach to the news, and their self-perception must all change if they want to survive. A great number of professions typically linked to the evolution of journalism have disappeared or are about to do so. I am not thinking here only of printers, who today are in charge of the quality control of rotary presses, or editors and proofreaders of nonexistent proofs. In a world where readers can use their cell phones to take photos and immediately send them to editorial offices or television stations, the role of press photographers will surely change. Digital technologies not only do things better, cheaper, and quicker, they also offer the opportunity for innovation. The aforementioned suggests that newspapers, as we have known them for the past couple of centuries, no longer possess the same meaning as before.

I have often asked the directors and editors of *El País* why stock market quotes or weather forecasts are included when such information is readily available through cell phones. What happened to journalism's famous rule of getting the news first? Today everything is broadcast live on the Internet. When the *New York Times* suffered a six-month strike in the 1980s due to job cuts at the rotary presses, television anchormen complained that they missed the newspaper's front page, as it helped them establish an order and hierarchy in the news and determine what was important. This connection enabled the newspaper to make a successful return to the newsstands once the trade unions lost the strike. A similar outcome would not occur today. Television, the Internet, and cell phones are the dominant modes of conveying the news.

The survival of the news, its influence on the behavior of citizens, and the central place it occupies in social organizations are all guaranteed by digital technology. However, the survival of newspapers is not. The Internet is not a newspaper. Newspapers are not on the Internet. The news on the Internet might be more enriching and varied than a traditional newspaper, but it cannot replace some of its essential functions.

A newspaper is a somewhat closed microcosm, a view of the world, a specific weltanschauung that cannot be reproduced in such a convergent, fragmented, and ambiguous universe as the Internet. The community of readers that sits around reading the newspaper has behaviors, sensitivities, and attitudes different from those of network communities. A loyal reader maintains a devotion, solidarity, and commitment to his newspaper that cannot be compared to those of a website visitor. However, journalists continue to approach the Internet as if it were still governed by the rules of the analog world.

Obsessed by our publication's print runs and circulation figures, we believe that our success online will be similarly dependent on the number of users our digital masthead is able to attract. It will take us some time to understand that if we want the values of traditional journalism (rigor, independence, credibility) to survive on the Internet, we must defend them in complete disregard for the number of users accessing our website. The deep relationship established between a traditional newspaper and its readers is impossible to duplicate digitally. Maybe the secret to newspaper survival lies here, provided that the printing press can shed its remaining heavy industry traits, as it did with hot lead typesetting and Linotype machinery, and adopt a production model more in tune with modern times.

One of the problems of the online versions of traditional newspapers is their meager economic return compared to the high margins of the printed paper. This not only represents a source of concern for newspaper owners and businessmen, but also an obstacle to quality improvements in digital systems. Fewer profits mean limited investments in human capital, which are necessary to guarantee a minimum standard in content. The best example of this is Google News, where machines are in charge of assessing the value of news items on the Net. Today, it is the leading information system in terms of number of users, and the one that has invested the least in the rigor, importance, or quality of the news. The lack of a business model capable of translating the positive experiences of the printed press into the online world reveals that we are still in the early days of this new era, and it explains why media companies focus their strategies on growth, convinced that volume is the only adequate answer to profitability requirements.

However, these strategies must consider the legal limits to concentration. Arguments favoring competition have taken on picturesque traits. Despite being highly regulated, the television sector is witnessing the ascendancy of transnational oligopolies, which are more than welcome by local political authorities. The arrival of telecommunications companies with a long, worldwide monopolistic tradition will subject the media market to additional pressures; we have already witnessed this in Spain. In any case, it's ridiculous to copy U.S. regulatory practices in markets that are much smaller. Experience has shown that if large conglomerates are capable of respecting the independence of journalists and content creators, they can coexist with freedom. The problem lies not so much in avoiding concentration but in limiting its negative aspects and guaranteeing the pluralistic flow of ideas. Attention to a global market requires egalitarian and homogenized content. The creation of a universal awareness or imagery, originating in the West, often clashes with traditions and customs from well-established cultures that feel invaded and violated by foreign trends. We still do not know how Islam or China will be affected by the multiplication of information sources brought by digital culture. We could assume that transforming the current regime in Iran would be easier through these methods than through armed action or popular pressure, but the abusive invasion of Iraq by the Anglo-American coalition revealed that the prevailing school of thought in the more technologically advanced countries is not always consistent with the new paradigm.

New media companies struggle with globalization. The

market's smaller segments will be populated by medium-sized companies that, in association with large conglomerates, combine the universal character of their content with the parochial tastes of their end users. These are the reasons for the numerous alliances between content creators and distributors; between those devoted to the development of artificial intelligence and Hollywood professionals; between telephone companies and information producers. Some of these alliances attempt to create synergy between partners, while others are geared toward gaining access to foreign markets, or as a defense against prospective competitors. There are also global companies that partner with much smaller enterprises in order to penetrate local markets. Such operations are determined by technological needs, capital requirements, and geostrategic concerns. On the other hand, the difficulties faced by the management of large conglomerates may aid smaller organizations, whose habits and decisions are closer to the tastes and needs of their clients and users. The amount of information and services provided by the digital world prefigures the rise of middlemen, who will pick and choose content according to the needs of specific markets.

The presence of multinational corporations in all

spheres of information and culture generates an inexorable trend toward homogenization. The establishment of English as our civilization's lingua franca parallels the spread of fast food (or plastic food) and Hollywood films as central elements of our collective identity as world citizens. Not everything in this realm is negative: the expansion of human rights and the observance of individual liberties and democratic values can help citizens of countries oppressed by dictatorships that seek justification through economic growth, ignoring other principles. It is necessary to draw a distinction between what democratic consciousness can tolerate in the name of a community's historic or folkloric peculiarities and what is unacceptable no matter how much a habit reflects prized local traditions or customs. The media can help check power, a role that is an intrinsic part of its history, and provide examples of freedom, a necessary condition for enjoying technological development and economic growth.

Democratic values are permanent, entrenched in history. New technologies often ignore these values. Privacy, a prerequisite for democracy, is increasingly violated by the digital generation, who are dazzled by the pretense that collective rights contradict individual freedom or are superior to it. The notion of history as accumulated progress is now questioned, and some intellectual groups and many circles of power celebrate its demise, hardly concealing their satisfaction.

The media must strive to preserve lasting values of democracy in the face of the ambiguities threatening those values. We face an increasingly complex and unpredictable world. Anti-globalization movements and the Porto Alegre challenge to Davos reveal how globalizing technologies enable and empower opposition. The enormous demonstrations against the invasion of Iraq were organized in a nearly autonomous manner to occur almost simultaneously around the world. All this was possible thanks to the Internet, which was despised by so many of the participants in these demonstrations. Once again, these examples show the universe of paradoxes and turning points that we face in the digital information society. The destiny that awaits us is one where we must learn to choose the right direction and live with a great number of contradictions. Such is the new meaning of risk in the immediate future.

SPEAKING IN TONGUES

"EACH DAY, THE prodigious advancement of the sciences and arts, the diffusion of intellectual culture, and political revolutions demand new ways to express new ideas; and the introduction of new words, taken from old and foreign languages, no longer offends us," wrote Andrés Bello in 1847, in the introduction to his work *Gramática*. Intended for use in the budding republics of America, today Bello's *Gramática* is the embodiment of Castilian as a universal language, and an early indication of its adaptable nature and ability to adjust to changing times and the demands of progress.

Language, like information, is the raw material with

which journalists work. We write thousands of pages and utter millions of words during our careers, not always with proper reflection. How we use language is often how our readers use language, due to the influence of what is supposedly a cultured class. Although I don't share the grief of my colleague and friend Fernando Lázaro Carreter about the dreadful influence of the media on language, I must acknowledge that the prosodic infidelities committed by broadcasters and columnists represent a considerable threat to the proper use of Spanish.

I once had the opportunity to discuss this subject in a memorable lunch with Lázaro Carreter, who at the time was the director of the Royal Academy, and José Ramón de la Morena, one of Spain's most well-known sports radio commentators. In the course of our conversation, one that has been had thousands of times throughout the world, I'm sure, it became clear to us that the issue of language is not a merely aesthetic or formal problem, but rather one that affects thought and reasoning in public opinion. Our thoughts are influenced by the words used to convey them, and this problem concerns journalists as much as academics, perhaps more so.

Language distinguishes us from other animals in the kingdom. It allows humans to express feelings, thoughts, sensations, and perceptions, to communicate and perceive another person's reality; language enables interior monologues, or even dialogues, as well as transcendent states. "He who talks alone wishes to talk to God some day," said Machado.

Reasoning is at the heart of expression, as are emotions. Language identifies humans as social beings, because they communicate with one another; on the other hand, language enables abstraction and helps define concepts, thoughts, and feelings. According to Genesis, Creation is bound up in language—or rather *logos*: In the beginning was the word. Perhaps this is the reason for the arrogance of many self-centered radio and television hosts, whose self-righteousness is matched only by God's after Creation.

While the creation of the world cannot be attributed to the phenomenon of language, the invention of culture is due almost exclusively to it. Arnold Toynbee marveled at the fact that the divine punishment of the arrogant inhabitants of Babylon, intent on building a tower to the heavens, consisted precisely in the confusion of languages. This is at least as revealing as the Holy Ghost's visit to the

Apostles during Pentecost, and the gift of speaking in tongues, without which all understanding and wisdom would have been useless.

Prior to the nineteenth century's Jacobin influence, nations and countries were defined by their languages, which represented both the origin of wars and the blossoming of cultures. Language represents the most powerful socializing agent in any community (even more so than weapons or money). It is therefore not surprising that many people defend their native tongue as the essential element of identity. Paradoxically, what originated as an instrument for communication and socialization has become a flag or banner, even a political grievance. If a language becomes the essential part of one's identity, it is precisely due to its unifying nature as a means or system of dialogue. But it is also an assertion of the individual's (or group's) own sovereignty. Since people think, believe, fear, and love in their own language, Wittgenstein dared to assume that the limits of existence are those of language.

Spanish is trendy, at least abroad. In Spain, awkward conventions on what is politically correct have led us to avoid this term, "Spanish," to designate our language. Has anyone ever seen a sign in London or New York that says, "Castilian Spoken Here"? And if such were the case, would the Ecuadorians, Argentines, Mexicans, Paraguayans, and so many other Spanish speakers understand that such a sign was referring to their own language? This question is illustrative of the language disputes in Spain, where these conflicts represent the identity of some of its people, so often manipulated—in this realm as in others—by their leaders.

Latin Americans and Spaniards boast a common culture because we have a common language, tied to our motherland. According to anthropologist Edward Tylor, "Culture, or civilization, taken in its broad, ethnographic sense, is that complex whole which includes knowledge, belief, art, morals, law, custom, and any other capabilities and habits acquired by man as a member of society." According to this definition, culture is the fundamental cultivation of intellect, and affects man from a social perspective, as a member of a community. Hence, all cultures identify and unify a group, and become the expression of such a group (for instance, when we talk about corporate culture), but they also represent a *historical fact*: they develop over time and are transmitted from generation to generation.

Spanish, or Hispanic, culture has three basic roots: First, a European one based in religion, influenced by Romanization first and the Holy Roman Empire later. To a great extent, we are European because we are Christian, and as such we have inherited a tradition that comes from the Apostles. Such an unquestionable fact has led the pope in Rome and a considerable number of Catholic politicians to request that Christianity be noted as a distinguishing trait in the text of the European Constitution.

Second, more than 120 million Muslims live in European Union countries, and thus the continent also has been nourished by Islamic roots, not only in history, but through geographic proximity and the mixing of Iberian peoples with Arabs.

And lastly, there is an American root that begins with the Spanish conquest and is consolidated in a common language, originally a Romance language derived from Latin, and distinguished by extensive Arab contributions and, later on, words from Indo-American tongues (Guaraní, Quechua, Nahuatl, and so many others). Though it was initially imposed by the empire, and despite being subject to so many different influences, the unity of the Spanish language was guaranteed by the Royal Academy of Language and its sister academies in Latin America.

These academies were created during the independence movements of the new republics so that political fragmentation wouldn't lead to language fragmentation. It is amazing to see how these civil institutions have willfully remained independent from political power, thereby guaranteeing the unity of Spanish language, which today represents the main cultural heritage of each and every one of our peoples. A single grammar, a single orthography, and a single dictionary for all Spanish speakers are the best guarantees of the strength of our cultural community and offer an opportunity to establish global communication systems and media, at least in Spanish.

The Royal Academy of Language acts as a notary public for language, but it is also in charge of prescribing its normative use—a responsibility that does not derive from political authority, but rather from the academy's social and scientific prestige. Attempts made by governments to manipulate languages—any language—are usually embarrassing and mostly doomed to failure, despite some occasional precarious success. Such interventions can only be maintained coercively, through threat of violence. The French experience is illustrative. The *francophonie* cannot be defended exclusively through the legislative assembly or the government's offices. Language is created by the people, not by legislators or ministers, but whether a language might be imposed and extended by an empire represents a separate issue. In the case of Castilian/Spanish we are witnessing a swift expansion despite a lack of support by political or economic power. Along with English and Mandarin Chinese, Spanish represents one of the three languages that will dominate in the immediate future.

The history of culture is also the history of limits and conflict. Political power relies on cultural power and uses it with worrying eloquence, to the point of rejecting the rights or even the lives of the people. This creates a breeding ground for confrontation and civil war, and many such wars have started when ethnic or religious minorities attempt to confront the so-called dominant culture, that is, the culture of whoever is in power. Experience has shown that all cultures often consider themselves the central reference point for the other cultures. Such attitudes were adopted centuries ago in China—the self-appointed Central Empire—Greece, Rome, the Catholic Church...

Napoleon and Hitler believed in the eminence of their cultures, and so has the United States, in an equally dogmatic fashion. The invading culture always assumes it will improve the culture of the invaded country; its agents are convinced that they represent loftier values and principles. Oppression is just one step further, and the line is fuzzy; to a great extent, this is the tale of Spain's domination of America. In one way or another, dominant cultures have always perceived themselves as global cultures, since they believe they are superior, more advanced, and, hence, worthy of expansion. Obviously, this is not always the case. Culturally, the barbarian rule of Europe represented an important step backward when compared to the Roman Empire, and the same can be said of the Spanish Reconquista compared to Islam during the Renaissance.

The expansion of culture has always been linked to the expansion of commerce. It was not by chance that the discovery of America and the invention of printing occurred almost simultaneously. The combined consequences of both phenomena changed the course of history. Today the rapid adoption of the digital ethos will yield similar results. We are facing an innovation that will change our lives as much as Gutenberg's invention changed the lives of our ancestors.

The dominant culture of the future—and even of

today—is the Web culture, which has been imposed not by weapons but by technology. The change is affecting language in the conventional way people relate to each other, favoring the extension of English and the newer, more specialized computer-related language, which is full of concepts, ideas, and representations that will have a profound effect on how we think.

Octavio Paz said that language gives us the feeling and the awareness of belonging to a community. The feeling of belonging to cyberspace also has its language, computer language—so iconographic at times—which we use to navigate the Internet, and an acolyte, English. Spanish, a language in continuous and autonomous expansion that shares a border with English along the Rio Grande and with Portuguese along the Iberian Lusitania frontier and also in the remote Amazonian jungles, will have to come to terms with this new reality.

Digital society threatens to destroy the unity of our language. There is a noticeable increase in the use of anglicisms, with the subsequent problems they entail, particularly in technical and scientific vocabulary. However, in this realm as in others, Castilian has proved highly flexible. If a Latin American hears that somebody has bought an *ordenador personal* (personal computer, in Spain), he might believe it is a machine that gives out orders, or even better, a system for classifying books, notes, or any other object. Spain is the only Spanish-speaking country where computers are not called *computadoras* (from the English *computer*, but also from the Latin *computare*). The reason for this difference is arbitrary. The first computers to arrive in Spain, the famous electronic brains, were brought by IBM via their French branch. The French have a completely independent terminology for computer development, where digital is translated as *logiciel*, and the computer is *l'ordinateur*. The instruction booklets for these first computers were translated from French into Spanish, without using the original English text. Hence, the success of the term *ordenador* among Spaniards.

If we consider the invasion of Castilian by the vocabulary of cyberculture, this anecdote seems to come straight from a science fiction novel. You don't need to be an *internauta* to know it is possible to *chat* or have a *blog* on the Web using Windows and Explorer applications, and that by going *clic* on the *ratón* (mouse) we can enjoy the benefits of *hipertexto*, provided we have enough *megas*. The number of digital terms we have directly incorporated into Spanish is enormous, beginning with *hardware* and *software*, continuing with *bit*, and on to *messenger*. Spanish has no choice but to accept these words, along with ensuing discussions about their orthography. The abundance of onomatopoeia and acronyms, so common in English and in the basic vocabulary of teenagers who spend so much time on the Internet, does not offer any help in the unification and normalization process of Spanish. However, the mistreatment of language by Internet users is not limited to Spanish. The deformities in Shakespeare's mother tongue are equally impressive.

The attacks on Spanish that originate in the orthographic versions of digital technology are not limited to the elimination of the tilde in the letter *ñ*—without which it is impossible to write *español* (Spanish) or *España* (Spain). Accents and punctuation marks are also among its victims, not to speak of the thesauruses and grammar aids incorporated into some programs, and which I emphatically recommend avoiding.

Automatic translation systems—based on the unlikely and undesirable existence of a neutral Spanish, created in the artificial environment of Hollywood dubbing studios—are not much better. However, the existing dangers and setbacks in this field are nothing compared to the threats that lie ahead if no prior agreement is reached on the use of voice recognition systems. The issue is not a matter of how computers will listen—they recognize all accents—but how they will speak to us. In the case of Castilian, more than 80 percent of its speakers use *ceceo* (the enunciation of *z* and *c* as an s when they come before an *i* or *e*), despite it being excluded from Spanish formal orthodoxy.

The need for rules that can recognize regional phonetic and pronunciation peculiarities does not preclude the existence of generally accepted principles that may safeguard the unity of our language. This task requires the consideration of language as a whole, and acknowledging that Spanish is not the private property of my fellow countrymen, when we barely represent 10–12 percent of the total Spanish-speaking population. The Castilian language is in no way the exclusive or essential property of Spaniards; hundreds of millions of Latin Americans possess the language as their mother tongue, too.

The influence of digital revolution on the evolution of our language is expanding. In developed countries, the printed press is trending downward, even in good times; the same with traditional books. Yet we shouldn't be alarmed as long as writing per se continues to be valued above oral expression and images to convey complicated ideas, to transmit knowledge. With respect to the anglicisms currently used in our language, the media bears the brunt of responsibility because many neologisms originate in the technical world, in economics, and in sports, and are subsequently sent out into the world, as it were.

We need an agreement on reliable translations, for *cash flow*, for example, a term everyone understands. Criticism about the crude Spanish spoken in the United States is widespread, as for instance when someone discusses a vaccination shot (from vacuum the carpet = *vacunar la carpeta*). But no one is shocked when bankers, businessmen, and ministers discuss *break-even* points and *jet lag*. The term *airbag* is already in the dictionary in Spain.

The dilution of languages is inevitable. In Mexico you take a *regaderazo* (shower, from *regadera*, watering can). It does not mean you have been hit by a watering can. And Latin Americans already know that *coger un taxi* does not mean having sex with a machine (from *coger*, to have sexual intercourse, in Latin America).

The nomenclature of technical innovation is imported by all Spanish-speaking countries; therefore, it is imperative that we all agree on univocal definitions. We can't assume this will take care of itself. If we do so, "neutral" Spanish, as mentioned earlier, becomes neutered language, created in a laboratory. No Spanish-speaking community recognizes or identifies with neutral Spanish. This neutered language serves the media and the media alone; it does not exist in academia, and it does not exist in government.

The Mexican American, Cuban, Puerto Rican, and Dominicano communities appear fragmented yet remain close to their places of origin. "Latin" continues to be a confusing, ambiguous concept and yet nobody can deny it describes a thriving reality, despite the fact that the very concept of Latin America, so prevalent in everyday language and so closely linked to the revolutionary representations and idealizations of the 1960s, is hardly observable in the sentiments and collective behavior of the many peoples that compose it. This might be due to the fact that Latin America is not a continent, as many believe, but an archipelago.

This is good news in the era of the Internet. The sea unites different lands more than it separates them, provided one knows how to sail and is willing to make the trip. The Hispanic community in the United States is becoming the most relevant island in the Latin American archipelago, more so than the great countries (Mexico, Argentina, Colombia), while Brazil is emerging as a remarkable power in which Spanish will soon be co-official. As a result of compulsory teaching, more than 12 million Brazilians will study Spanish in 2010. The transatlantic community of Spanish speakers is much more than a fantasy or rhetoric (even though rhetoric and liturgy continue to be important). The Internet and the media must be the preferred vehicles for the unification of this community.

The cultural, historical, and political roots of the Hispanic community in the United States represent a different issue. Global Spanish speakers must achieve solidarity and unification in North America; they must, as a group, have valid identity codes. Very few among them know that the first city founded by Europeans in what is now the United States was St. Augustine, Florida. The conquest and colonization of California has yet to be understood by Spanish-speaking Americans; ditto the adventures of Hernándo de Soto in the southeast. Even the Cuban presence in Tampa, Florida, which predated the Cuban nationals who fled Fidel Castro and which is linked to the bourgeoisie's rejection of Spanish rule of the island, is scarcely valued by Floridians.

The roots of Hispanic Americans go back further than the adventures of so-called wetbacks, the anti-Castro exiles, or recent emigrants from Puerto Rico. Hispanic Americans must take pride in being among the founders of North America, as opposed to refugees or fugitives; such status is not alien, marginal, or borrowed, but rather something that has endured for centuries. Everything has been accomplished with and through language, and today it represents the main link—beyond citizenship, ethnicity, and social class—to a common fatherland.

Those of us who believe that Spanish symbolizes and embodies the essence of the Hispanic community, and who understand and promote the strength that lies in its unity, must make an effort to supply a network of content in Spanish. A common language represents a common culture as well as shared origins and destinies. It is also an invaluable instrument for promoting mutual understanding, intellectual development, and scientific progress, as well as the only way of freeing people from oppression, misery, and ignorance.

LIFE IN A BLOG

DR. NICOMEDES GUTIERREZ was a rural doctor who used to keep a detailed diary of his daily routine. In love with the village teacher, he decided to have a bachelor party before marrying her. He enjoyed an outrageous night out and recorded the details in his diary. With such simple elements, playwright Carlos Llopis created a bedroom farce that was turned into a film titled *La vida en un bloc* (*Life in a Notebook*).

The film featured Fernando Rey and José Luis Ozores, along with other mythical Spanish movie actors, and the role of Dr. Nicomedes was played by Alberto Closas. As a teenager I remember sneaking into the cinema to watch the movie—it was rated R—but I remember little else, apart from the title and the vague reference about the plot that I have just outlined.

For my generation, a *bloc* is a group of paper sheets glued or sewn together at one edge that is used to take notes, although it works best as a book in which to doodle during boring meetings. *Bloc* has English origins, but etymologists think it entered Spain via France, and they must be right, since among the many meanings of the word in Webster's dictionary none refer to a notebook or a group of paper sheets. In any case, the word *bloc* is an example of our language's intercultural effort to adapt; it was included in the Royal Academy's dictionary decades ago and is as Spanish as any other word.

Another recently imported neologism is *blog*, which has been unsuccessfully translated as *bitácora* (logbook). Had Dr. Nicomedes lived today, he surely would not have been a rural doctor, for they no longer exist. And he would not have written about his life on a *bloc*, but rather in a blog, which hasn't yet found its way into our dictionary in Spain. It was chosen as "word of the year" in 2004. Perhaps by the time this book has been translated and published in the English-speaking world, *blog* will have appeared in some dictionaries here in Spain.

Despite its enormous popularity, the term *blog* is a neologism in English: it is less than ten years old, yet it took only five years to grow up, in a sense. Statistics indicate that more than 100 million blogs exist; 1,000 new ones are created every day, one every minute and a half. There are 400 million blog users. Despite such popularity, those of us who do not use the Internet have difficulty understanding what a blog is. For these readers I will explain that a blog is nothing more than a personal diary on the Web. Such a diary can be either personal or collective, and thanks to the system's connectivity it ends up being a place for communication, a new form of socialization typical of cyberspace; a common ground that, among other things, defies the classical notion of politics as the management of common public space.

According to experts, it was a journalist named Justin Hall who pioneered the innovation. When Justin was a twenty-year-old college student he started using his Web page daily, surfing the Internet and writing. He then got a job at *Wired*. Anybody who digs further into this underwhelming biography of a young pioneer of new technologies will learn that his craft, both as a writer and as the inventor of the blog, was strongly influenced by the suicide of his alcoholic father when Justin was seven years old, as well as by his involvement with *Wired*'s editorial team.

Blogs differ from traditional diaries in at least two essential ways: in a traditional diary all entries are made in chronological order; in a blog this order is reversed, so the first entry we read is the newest one, and from there we go back in time as we read. The second and more important difference is that, in general, diaries are devoted to our innermost secrets. Stationery stores still sell booklets that can be locked. Blogs are intended to be read, and they are full of links to other blogs; privacy is not among the values they pretend to defend or stand for. Instead, they seem to share a passion for exhibitionism, which is common to the Web under the pretext of communication. In the end, those who expose themselves on the street are also trying to communicate.

Justin Hall was followed by others. In 1997, when the system was not yet fully developed, Jorn Barger used the term *Weblog* (a log on the Web) for his site. Two years later Peter Merholz, who set up a page under the narcissistic name *Peterme*, broke up the word into "we blog," thus creating both a noun and a verb. Those willing to translate the term into Spanish found that *log*, among other meanings, is any method of registering events during sea or air travel, and *logbook* is the English equivalent of *cuaderno de bitácora*, which was originally adopted by Spanish speakers to designate a blog. Since the term was too lengthy it was shortened to *bitácora*, which is still used today. However, *bitácora* is the wooden structure that houses the compass on a ship, next to the rudder. So the term does not seem to be very fitting to the open, communicative space of blogs, where the compass seems to experience an irrepressible inclination to go crazy.

Thus, at the next meeting of the Royal Academy of Language I will submit a request for the elimination of italics (which denote a term's foreign origin) in the Spanish writing of blog. This is surely what needs to be done, ditto for blogger, "to blog," or blogosphere. I suggest this because we must call things by their names. The Academy has always observed this rule, which only attempts to contribute to the construction of our language, as opposed to the destruction that is carried out by others, especially our political class. Murdering orthography is not a prerequisite to winning an election.

The creation of new words on the Internet is endless. Nearly all neologisms in Spain are either abbreviations or English words, although the preeminence of English in cyberspace is increasingly challenged by Chinese. In the blogosphere, English has been overtaken by Japanese, which is used by nearly 40 percent of the world's bloggers, as opposed to 37 percent for English and barely 3 percent for Spanish. The difficulty that the Spanish language faces in establishing its presence in scientific and technical vocabulary has not vanished; it has, in fact, been amplified.

One of the traits of the Internet culture is that knowledge is developed and enhanced in a cooperative and global manner, not by a solitary scholar in a laboratory or in the small departments of reputed universities. The ensuing paradox is the frequency with which young people, almost teenagers, make revolutionary discoveries in their garages or university dorms. Bill Gates is a well-known example. Online communities, a new way of socializing for young people, are created by other young people with barely any means or theoretical knowledge; however, they know the behavior and habits of their peers and immature adults.

One of the most blatant violations of the rules of language derived from everyday technological devices is the disregard of orthography in cell phone texting. Sometimes for the sake of economy in time and space, or for just plain economy, a multitude of signs and symbols, which display a lack of any observance of orthographic rules and disdain for syntax, threaten to mold an uneducated and confused generation, attached to instant messaging and with little inclination for reading and thinking.

We must not forget that we talk like we think because we think like we talk. The articulation of language is connected to the articulation of the mind. The academic world should pay closer attention to the erosion of language resulting from cell phone applications. Likewise, it should not accept users as the sole source for establishing norms and linguistic equivalences in the Rosetta stone of our language.

We need to work with users to create and establish a language appropriate for chats and texting. A dictionary and orthography, and perhaps even its own grammar, must be created that helps understand the interactivity between digital and analog languages, and prevents the destruction of the latter by mobloggers (moblogs are blogs with images and even videos, sent through cell phones. Since their activity is still embryonic, we can spare the inclusion of the term in the dictionary for the time being).

Despite the likely damages to language caused by digital networks, I do not believe that the frivolity of such exchanges is cause for concern. Superficiality can be an attractive element of conversation, whether at a bar, at the dinner table, or even on a radio talk show. It's unreasonable to demand that teenagers maintain a deeper level of dialogue on the Internet than in conversations on the street or at home. On the other hand, dressing up frivolity in respectable clothes, the resounding vacuity of demagogues, and the credulity awarded to liars and charlatans is worrying. All of these problems are especially evident today.

The Internet is an immense construction of words, a global conversation flowing in all directions, where the act of speaking, of communicating, is often more important than the content itself. Many bloggers have a peculiar way of addressing readers, a sort of participative reporting, which reminds me of some of the good qualities of the journalist's craft and which suggests a new genre, already defined by communication theorists as "conversational information."

Of the millions of active bloggers, only a minority

inhabits the role of the journalist as middleman, the conveyor of information and news; most are agitators or promoters of innuendo. Undoubtedly this is the reason for so much information. From the blogger's point of view, as well as from the "citizen's journalism" perspective, it represents a contribution to the development of participatory democracy, whatever that may be.

While the world of communication in general and printed press in particular continues to be analog, it will continue to behave simultaneously as a cause and a consequence of political representation systems. Newspapers are as old, or as young, as representative democracy, and share its fate. Neither journalists nor political leaders seem aware of this reality. Journalists are obsessed with independence, and politicians with manipulating it. However, the digital effect on the media and the development of the Internet have resulted in the blurring of what lies at the center, politically, and what lies on the margins. The lack of hierarchies and the chaos also have a place in the new digital culture; such qualities are antithetical to the hierarchical nature of modern societies.

In May 2008 the shares of Apple plummeted when the Engadget blog announced a delay in the launching of the iPhone, the latest trendy gizmo, a cross between a phone and a music player. The news, or "clip," as they say in blog jargon, turned out to be false, created by some hackers posing as Apple employees.

Hackers have been worrisome for some time, beginning with the translation of the term into Spanish. We used to call them "electronic pirates," but piracy is something different, and in any case buccaneers would never board a ship to leave a gift, however malicious it may be. The rights and values of our legal system and social behavior tend to vanish in the information society. Property and privacy are losing credibility.

The first details of the Sichuan earthquake were transmitted via Twitter, when traditional media still struggled to establish communication. One of Twitter's most common programs allows instant communication with hundreds of thousands of people by asking the simple question, "What are you doing now?" Answering this question has become the rage. The inventor of the system, in which users can access the network from even the simplest cell phones, had previously revolutionized the use of publishing tools in the blogosphere. He seems to be following suit with the construction of social networks on the Internet.

One can now follow a person's life through text and video from the moment he wakes up in the morning until bedtime. A company in California invites users to film their lives and broadcast them live. Television's *Big Brother* has nothing on personal reality shows. In the first two weeks, the website attracted half a million viewers and streamed 18,000 hours of video. This begs the question whether Céline's famous saying is still relevant: "Everything interesting takes place in the shadow. The true history of man is unknown." And we can wonder about the future of neologisms originating on the Web, some of which I have mentioned several times. If such applications thrive, we will soon be able to *tweet* each other, and *tweeting* will then represent something quite different from being on a first-name basis.

We use words to name reality, but they can also be useful in transforming it. Our lives will change significantly as we incorporate the terms we have been discussing into our vocabulary and behavior. Not a single corner of the future society will be spared. Culture and the means through which it is transmitted evolve swiftly, and the effects of new technologies on the evolution of language and thought require special attention by our best minds, our best leaders. Today, virtually all existing knowledge

JUAN LUIS CEBRIÁN

is on the Internet, available to whoever has adequate technology and the education to access it. Our development and well-being, as well as the globalization of culture, depend on how sensitive we are to digital innovations, however unintelligible they might seem at the moment.

NEWSPAPER WRITERS

SINCE ITS INCEPTION, journalism has been a genre of literature, and its history is full of great chroniclers who also wrote literature, literary essays, poetry, short stories, and so on. I am referring not only to published novels as serials in newspaper and magazines, but also to the journalist/novelist's combined skills as a reporter, columnist, critic, and commentator. The nineteenth century is full of such writers, beginning with Charles Dickens. Today it is impossible to imagine the lives of such writers as Hemingway, García Márquez,

Camus, or Vargas Llosa without considering their activities as editorialists, correspondents, special envoys, or even typesetters.

For Whom the Bell Tolls would never have been written had Hemingway not been a war correspondent in Spain. Camus founded and ran a newspaper, *Combat*, which collaborated with other publications like *L'Express*. He was active in the journalistic craft, and often thought about the craft:

> If writers had the minimum consideration for their profession they would be very choosy about where their work is published. But it seems that one must accommodate, and in order to please others, one must give in. Let us speak clearly: it is obviously difficult to launch a frontal attack against those machines that make and break reputations. When a newspaper, however contemptible it may be, has a circulation of six hundred thousand copies, far from insulting its director, we invite him over for dinner. However, our mission is not to fall for that false complicity. Our honor depends on the energy we devote to avoiding commitment.

After winning the Nobel Prize in Literature, Gabriel García Márquez returned to work as a reporter, not only in his admirable book *News of a Kidnapping*, but also in his lively chronicles for the Spanish and Colombian press on such subjects as the Lewinsky affair or Hugo Chávez's trips to Cuba. As for Vargas Llosa, I have repeatedly told the story of how I once had his job at the French Press agency in the old Parisian building at 13 Place de la Bourse, in 1964. He had just received an award for *The Time of the Hero* and saw an opportunity to focus on his novels. As I wrote these lines he was working in the Congo as a special envoy.

Well over the age of fifty, José Saramago abandoned his career as a journalist for that of the novelist after being sacked as editor of a Lisbon newspaper. Graham Greene did something similar, weary of working as chief editor for a London newspaper. The list of writers, reporters, and newspaper editors who are or became creative writers is unending.

Literature, like life, is diverse. There are many lives and many ways of being a writer. Nobody is excluded from trying more than one form, and there is no shame in doing so. We know of great authors who had a natural talent for journalism, and famous journalists who tried their luck at writing novels. Some have left us and others continue working away, but they all are exemplars for today's youth.

Dickens is surely the most celebrated of all. One of the creators of the modern novel was a journalist his entire life, whether as a reporter, a parliamentary chronicler, or an editor at the *Daily News*. The rough humor of *The Pickwick Papers* and the bitter descriptions of the English underworld of poverty and debtors' jail reveal the satirical audacity of a critic and the expressive perception of a journalist. Far from the figure of the wretched or marginalized intellectual, Dickens exemplified the successful and influential writer who nonetheless refused to submit to so-called higher authorities and who broadcast his convictions and understanding of life, very much in line with the ideas expressed by Albert Camus.

As with Camus, the mundane aspects of Dickens's life, sometimes tinged with frivolity, contribute to his appeal. Charles Dickens was not a thinker, but a storyteller, an observer, and a man convinced of the entertaining quality of literature. He also embodied the professional constraints of a journalist. He was pragmatic and dedicated to the craft of journalism. This is obvious in his exceptional narrative rigor, an admirable deference to facts taken at an often ironic distance, and a hard-nosed approach to language.

Considering the frequent representations of journalism as a minor genre of literature, a subgenre, or even something unrelated to it, the example set by Dickens is comforting to those of us who believe that institutional distinctions between art and entertainment are false distinctions created for the comfort of those under the comforter. *The Pickwick Papers* is among his most popular novels and brought Dickens widespread acclaim and recognition. It can be considered part of what today is called the comic culture, or *manga*, as it is known in Japan.

Dickens had initially been asked to write dialogue for the scripts and drawings that the newspaper had commissioned Robert Seymour to create; in fact, Seymour claimed that *The Pickwick Papers* was his idea. This first attempt did not produce a cartoon, but rather a work that is exceptionally rich in nuance and situation, one that rivals the great monuments of world literature. The innovative disposition shown by the author of *Oliver Twist* appears in stark contrast to the reluctance shown by some supposedly great authors of our time toward forms of art and entertainment considered minor by the traditional canon.

The modern character of a society and its members is partly reflected in its attitude toward progress. The traditional resistance of so many Spanish writers and intellectuals toward new techniques and forms, toward the importance of entertainment—just barely overcome recently—and the predominant deference and sanctification of written culture over audiovisual culture is still burdensome. In order to be successful, a writer might have to wait until one of his novels is adapted for the big screen. What would people say if, instead of writing a novel, an author first imagines a television series, only to be published later as a book? Greene, Faulkner, and Pinter proved that a good script deserves as much recognition as a good novel or a successful drama. We now wait for the next literary success stories to be designed for distribution exclusively via cell phones.

Ever since the press came into existence, it is rare to find an important author who has never worked as a reporter or columnist. Carlos Fuentes who, at age eighty, continues to write frequently on international policy for newspapers, is still admirably prolific as a storyteller. Gabriel García Márquez is the most peculiar case. His professional career (from *El Universal* to *El Heraldo*, and then to *El Nacional de Barranquilla*, where he was chief editor, and finally to *El Espectador de Bogotá*) attests to his journalistic experience. This was clear in the short biography I published about him in 1989 for Círculo de Lectores.

While writing his own fiction, he has done interviews, news analysis, opinion columns, travel chronicles, and investigative journalism. He worked as a special envoy to Europe for the New York news agency *Prensa Latina*. In his youth he helped launch a magazine, *Crónica*, where he worked as chief editor; he also headed an alternative newspaper, *Comprimido*—testimony to his concise style, though it survived only six days. He was surely aware that synthesis was one of the values of modern journalism, something often forgotten by today's journalists. Amid concerns about decreasing circulation, editors publish hundreds of pages nobody reads, maybe because people are aware of Lord Thomson's saying: "As for editorial content, that's the stuff you separate the ads with." Unfortunately, advertising revenue is also declining.

Gabriel García Márquez loves newspapers. He used

his Nobel Prize award money to found a newspaper, *El Otro*. For months he traveled repeatedly to Madrid to meet with the staff at *El País* and discuss the concerns of creating a newspaper. He also sent his team of collaborators to different editorial offices in Europe. As implied by its name, *El Otro* (*The Other One*) attempted to publish news with a point of view at variance with the rest of the Colombian press. But it was never published. The Nobel Prize money proved insufficient.

It is impossible to imagine that the prose of *One Hundred Years of Solitude* and the exuberant ability to describe the indescribable that flows from its pages could have existed without the journalistic know-how of its author. Published in April 1955 in *El Espectador*, "The Story of a Shipwrecked Sailor" is another superb example of this ability. Over several episodes García Márquez recounted the memories of a sailor who survived the shipwreck of a navy destroyer. Today, critics and historians consider it a masterpiece.

While the barriers between journalism and literature are often invisible, in García Márquez's case their paths sometimes cross in obvious ways. His background in journalism provided him with sharp observation skills, a concern for his readers, and a desire not to turn writing into an act of narcissistic self-aggrandizing. He has always been a committed author, never hiding his personal or political loyalties, and has dedicated time and money to teaching film and journalism. He is the president of the Foundation for New Latin American Journalism, headquartered in Cartagena de Indias, and has been collaborating for decades with the Cuban Cinematographic Institute and the Havana Festival.

That journalism is a genre of literature does not mean that there are no boundaries between the two. Some dramatic differences exist, and they clearly establish journalism's role in relation to fiction, including historical novels or the description of facts. Some realities cannot be described without imagination. Journalistic rigor—based on hard facts, dates, quantities, proof—has nothing to do with novelistic rigor, which is anchored in anecdote and detail. In the novel, imagination and evocation are far more important than documents or statements in the transmission of reality—even if that reality exists only on paper or on a computer's liquid crystal display.

It takes a while for those journalists who write fiction to understand how to manage time. I refer here to the time involved in writing as well as the time that needs to be devoted to reading. In contrast to the urgent and perishable nature of chronicles, stories are mysteriously endowed with a vocation for durability and permanence. Only a master can blend elements in which the rigor of facts is combined with creative passion.

Two characteristics of creativity are solitude and the notion of difference. They are hardly compatible with the role of the journalist, who is subject to the hustle and bustle of an editorial office within an industrial system of standardized procedures. The genius of a journalist lies in those pieces written for a daily newspaper that immediately convey transcending qualities.

Just as a politician can convey his or her gifts through speeches that project enduring values and insights alien to the context in which they were given, the great newspaper writers are those who, like Mariano José de Larra, the nineteenth-century Spanish writer best known for his essays, are able to write criticism that transcends the genre. In Spain, Larra is the most obvious example of the sundry dealings among journalism, literature, and politics. He possessed a combination of bohemia and elegance, a fun-loving spirit and a reflexive genius; he inhabited the world of literature, of newspapers, of coffee and tobacco.

Larra was foremost a journalist, even though his newspaper articles preceded the industrial revolution and the modernization of the press. His style, his way of doing business, his relationship to his readers, his constant provocation, the success of his attitude and his lifestyle, all harmonized with his gifts as a journalist. An early representative of Spanish Romanticism, he did not have a poetic soul, but instead was endowed with deadly prose. Whoever was the target of his pen ended up impaled, instantly annihilated. Irony, sarcasm, and bitter criticism were his weapons, which are so often imitated by today's minions. His deeds remain unrivaled.

Reading Larra is important for anyone wanting to become a journalist, for a newspaper or for a website, whether writing chronicles or blogging. There hasn't been anyone better, sharper, or more accurate in observing the quotidian. Anyone doubting journalism as a literary genre should read a collection of articles by Figaro (the *nom de plume* of Larra) or *El pobrecito hablador*. Perhaps a few masterful sentences, like those devoted to the "balloon man," so dreadfully recognizable today, will suffice:

Come and see the balloon man with all his gifts! What ballyhoo! What heights he reaches! What fame, what prestige! He is going up now. Look how he ascends in the balloon that has been blown up especially for him. Who can doubt his gifts, his excellence? On earth we can touch his greatness, pomp, and fame. Yet as the balloon rises he seems smaller. When the balloon reaches the height of the Palace, which is not so great, it's already the size of a hazelnut, and the balloon man is nothing: a bit of smoke, a great but empty cloth. And of course, when the balloon gets up very high in the sky it is discovered that there is no set course. Is it possible that the balloon man doesn't know how to steer this balloon?

Maybe the only solution is to pop the balloon. That is what I have attempted to do with these essays: to destroy myths, to provoke discussion fit for whorehouses. After all, for many years whorehouses were more respectable in the eyes of the ruling class than the editorial offices of newspapers. Maybe this is the secret to survival in the digital revolution.

JUAN LUIS CEBRIÁN, is one of the original editiors of Spain's leading newspaper, *El Pais*, and its first director. He is currently the Managing Director of Prisa, Spain's leading media group, and a member of the board of directors of *Le Monde*. He has received Spain's National Journalism Prize, the Freedom of Expression Medal awarded by the F. D. Roosevelt Four Freedoms Foundation, and the Trento International Journalism and Communication Prize.

HAROLD EVANS, editor of the *Sunday Times* of London (1967–1981) and the *Times* (1981–1982), is also the author of *My Paper Chase* (2009), an autobiography.